Abducted to Oz

by

Chris Dulabone

Robert J. Evans

Abducted to Oz
by Chris Dulabone
Robert J. Evans

ISBN: 978-93-59951-19-5

Published by

DOUBLE 9 BOOKS

2/13-B, Ansari Road
Daryaganj, New Delhi – 110002
info@double9books.com
www.double9books.com
Tel. 011-40042856

ABOUT THE AUTHOR

Chris Dulabone and Robert J. Evans are completed authors whose collaborative efforts have yielded a numerous frame of work spanning numerous genres. Their collective literary skills have enriched the realms of fiction, non-fiction, and academic discourse, charming readers with their enticing narratives and thought-provoking insights. Chris Dulabone, recognised for his bright storytelling and deep exploration of characters, has contributed considerably to the arena of fiction. His narratives regularly combo factors of mystery, fantasy, and science fiction, developing immersive worlds and unforgettable adventures for readers. Robert J. Evans, alternatively, brings a wealth of understanding and knowledge to his non-fiction writing, in particular in fields including history, technology, and era. His works are characterised by meticulous research, clarity of expression, and a commitment to conveying complicated thoughts in a reachable way. Together, Dulabone and Evans have embarked on collaborative tasks that exhibit their versatility as authors. Their blended literary endeavors have resonated with a huge-ranging target market, reflecting their ardour for storytelling and their willpower to intellectual exploration. Whether thru charming fiction or insightful non-fiction, their contributions keep to depart a long-lasting mark on the sector of literature and scholarship.

CONTENTS

CHAPTER ONE
THE ABDUCTION

The boy was doing his homework. His parents had taken his little brother to see *Return to Oz* at the movie theater. He had seen it when it first came out and, although he enjoyed it at the time, he felt he was getting too old for that sort of stuff. Besides, he had too much work to do. It seemed to him that each teacher allocated enough work to practically take up a fellow's entire evening—as if their class was the only one. So Graham, for that was his name, knew he would have to work for several more hours if he was to complete all the assignments.

Graham began to work on his math problems, but he could not concentrate. His mind drifted off to the original L. Frank Baum story: *The Wonderful Wizard of Oz*. He was thinking about the characters in it and what a terrific imagination Mr. Baum must have had, when suddenly, out of the stillness of the house, came a weird screeching sound. The sound was like nothing he had ever heard before. It seemed to have come from behind him; from the vicinity of the fireplace. Graham shivered. He did not believe in ghosts, and at twelve years old (almost thirteen) he should not be afraid to be home alone. But he was scared right now—no question about it. However, when no other sound was forthcoming, he began to rationalize that it had all been his imagination, perhaps just the wind whistling down the chimney. Then it happened! The awful sound of breaking glass. "Oh no," he thought. "Someone is breaking in!" He looked over to the window—then to the French doors. Nothing! Yet the sound had seemed very close. He glanced at the mirror above the fireplace only to see that all the glass had gone, leaving an empty frame. Now he was really frightened. He wondered what had caused the glass to shatter. Then, to his amazement, all the pieces of slivered glass suddenly flew up from the fireplace and reconstructed themselves in the frame.

"I must be going crazy!" thought the poor lad. "All this school work is getting to be too much for me. I must have cracked completely!" Then all the lights in the house went out, leaving him in pitch blackness. At that moment there was a strange crackling sound, and the mirror became illuminated with a purple glow. A grotesquely human face began to form into the image of an evil Witch. A loud, screechy cackle emanated from her throat. It was the same sound he had heard earlier. By now Graham was absolutely frozen with fear.

The Witch's evil eyes glared at him as she screamed, "So, my little man. We meet at last. You have hated me ever since you first read about me, haven't you? HAVEN'T YOU?" she shouted. "ANSWER ME, YOU LITTLE BRAT!" She reached her arms out of the mirror, grabbed him, and shook him hard. She shook and shook until he thought he was going to be sick. Then she lifted him right up off the floor and into the mirror. By now Graham was absolutely terrified. He kicked and screamed and tried to escape, but to no avail. The Witch was much too strong for him. He found himself dragged to the other side of the mirror and out into a room in the Witch's castle, whereupon the Witch immediately released her grip, for she knew that the boy had nowhere to run.

"Well, what say you now, squirt? Do you still hate me?" cackled the Witch, breaking into fits of hideous laughter.

"Oh, no. Not anymore," replied Graham, his voice trembling. "I think you're pretty nice, um, all things considered."

"Oh, come now!" replied the Witch. "Let's be reasonable. You don't really think that. You're just afraid of what I might do to you. Look at you. You're shaking in your boots!"

"I'm afraid, yes," said Graham. "Really afraid. But I don't think you'll harm me after you hear what I have to say."

"Oh," replied the Witch. "Really? And what might that be?"

Graham knew he had piqued her interest and was now desperately trying to think of a plausible story that would keep her occupied while he tried to figure out a way to escape. He had managed to see out of one of her windows and knew he was, without a doubt, in the Land of Oz.

CHAPTER TWO
HISTORICAL BACKGROUND

Now, in the event that this book may have fallen into the hands of someone who is unfamiliar with the marvelous Land of Oz, it seems fitting that an explanation be inserted right about here. Oz is an oblong-shaped country that is surrounded on all sides by a vast Deadly Desert that is supposed to keep visitors out. Even so, it has been visited by any number of American children prior to Graham's visit. Some came by way of invitation, but mostly they arrived by accident. The most famous of these visitors, of course, was little Dorothy Gale. Dorothy traveled to Oz via a powerful cyclone which carried her house and herself over the massive desert and plopped her on top of a particularly evil Witch. With the help of a live Scarecrow, a man made out of tin, and a Cowardly Lion, she was able to find her way back to her home in America. She returned a short time later and had a wonderful new series of adventures in which she met Princess Saari, Gayelette, and even some Fuzzy Yellow Wogglebugs. It was but a few years after that when little Dorothy finally consented to become a citizen of Oz and live there happily—or reasonably so—for many years thereafter. In fact, even after nearly eighty-five years, she remains an honorary princess of that lovely country. Because no one has to ever grow old or die in this singular land, Dorothy remains as young and innocent as on the day she first arrived. At one point, Dorothy was joined by a fine young boy named Button-Bright, who was about as bright as a cloth-covered button. Trot Griffiths, Betsy Bobbin, and several others have also agreed to live the rest of their days in Oz rather than returning home to the mortal lands, where illness and death and aging are common.

Because Oz citizens only age when they wish to do so, on one's birthday all one is required to do is to wish to stay the same age for another year, and it will be so. This would certainly please most of the people in our mortal lands, but it would hardly be practical here due to the ever-increasing overpopulation problem.

The Land of Oz is divided into five sections. To the North is the Gillikin territory. The Gillikins favor the color purple above all others and are known to paint their homes, barns, and silos in this color. To the South lies the land of the Quadlings. Here, the revered color is red. The area is governed by a powerful but Good Witch named Glinda, and Glinda is considered an enemy to all of the evil Witches. The very center is the Emerald City. It has been called the most glorious place on the face of the earth (or even the moon or Mars), and rightly so. It is so lovely, in fact, that it defies description. And it is from here that the overall ruler is able to reign above all five regions.

In the West can be found the yellow Winkie Country. The Emperor of this region is none other than Nick Chopper, the tin man who had befriended Dorothy on her first visit to Oz. To the East is the blue Munchkin Country. Here, all of the things that the Gillikins paint purple are painted blue. This is the region where little Dorothy's house had fallen down atop the Wicked Witch of the East. And it was this incident that had caused the Wicked Witch of the West to take notice of the little girl. So wicked was this Witch, in fact, that she sent a host of plagues in the hope that they would destroy poor Dorothy and her companions. She lashed out with her flesh-eating gray wolves, her sinister crows, and her horrific stinging bees. But it was not until she called upon her Marvelous Flying Monkeys that she was able to succeed in her goal. The monkeys, enslaved by the powers of a magical hat, destroyed the Scarecrow and tin man and enslaved Dorothy and the Lion.

Oz history would have been dismal, indeed, had Dorothy not splashed a bucket of water over the Wicked Witch, wetting her from head to foot. As Witches and water do not mix very well, the evil woman was reduced to nothing more than a puddle of ugly liquid. With the help of some kindly Winkie tinsmiths and seamstresses, Dorothy was able to retrieve her friends and bring happiness back to Oz. Had she desired to live there then, she would have had a welcoming home with any or all of the citizens of Oz, even the Scarecrow, who was made ruler over all the land. The Scarecrow was a good and honest king—a thing that rarely happens in the mortal lands—but was not to stay long in that position. Instead, he had gladly handed over his crown to the rightful ruler of Oz, Princess Ozma. Even though she is but a child, Ozma has become the most well-loved ruler in all the earth. Citizens of Oz love her like a sister, while children of other countries who read Oz books yearn to leave their homes to go to that wonderful country to be near to her.

Of course, Oz is a very big place. But if all of us who wished to go there were suddenly whisked away on a cyclone of our own, it would surely become decidedly too crowded. So it is good for Oz that we are made to stay here except on the rare occasion when Ozma may call upon one of us, or one of us may find Oz by accident.

CHAPTER THREE
PRELUDE TO THE PARADE

Dorothy and Ozma have become fast friends over the many ageless years. Only on rare occasions is the incident with the Wicked Witch discussed any more. Once a year, on the day of the anniversary, there is a parade and a feast, but the reason for these festivities is not generally acknowledged. The very fact that dear little Dorothy is present is considered reason enough to celebrate. Oz people, it should be told, will accept any excuse to have a celebration. And the celebration might well have continued as it always had, except that something most peculiar had happened this year. Sir Simon the Shrew, who had come to live in the Emerald City after Princess Ozma had magically enlarged him to human-size, had become very good friends with Dorothy. He was of the opinion that the annual festival should better commemorate the event on which it was founded. He determined that the most elaborate float in the parade should be one which depicted Dorothy dousing the Wicked Witch with water.

Because he was now as large as a human child, Simon was able to gather together the materials he needed in record time. Although he was hardly W.W. Denslow or Frank Kramer, Simon's artistic abilities were far superior to those of Dirk. Borrowing the Red Wagon, he created a large platform on which he could build his float. He arranged with Kabumpo, the Elegant Elephant, to draw the float through the streets, as he thought it would be too heavy for the Sawhorse. Kabumpo agreed to this only because he respected Dorothy and because he enjoyed parades. He was still a tad disgruntled about being used as a work-horse, but he allowed this feeling to be repressed in favor of the pomp and circumstance of the parade. He was, after all, a bit of a show-off when he could get away with it. And that is a real understatement!

Sir Simon the Shrew was able to construct upon the Red Wagon a magnificent papier maché image that kind of resembled Dorothy. She wore one shoe, which Simon coated with glue and sprinkled with silver glitter. He deftly colored her dress blue and white and gave her two braids in her ribbon hair. He stood back and admired his masterpiece. "Wow!" said Simon. "This will get a lot of attention!" But he still had to make the Wicked

Witch. This was a harder prospect, as Simon did not like to create anything that was ugly. To be sure, there are very few people or things that are uglier than the Wicked Witch of the West.

After some time and not less than three failed attempts to construct a figure of the old Witch, Sir Simon sighed. It was hard to make her look right. Because of his kind and gentle nature, Simon's images always wound up looking too friendly. This was not the right image for the Wicked Witch at all. She had to look mean and hateful. She had to look like the kind of person who would happily have the Tin Woodman and the Scarecrow destroyed, or take an innocent little girl as her slave without remorse. At last, he decided he had to do it with his eyes closed. This way, he would not be as repulsed by the Witch's cruelty. Shutting his rodentine eyes, Sir Simon painted the most horrible face he could. After he opened his eyes to look at his handiwork, he found himself feeling quite queasy. He had to turn away to avoid being sick. "Perfect," he muttered. "It looks just like her."

He then set up the float and hinged the arms of the Dorothy figure in such a way that she could dump a bucket over the Witch's head. Giving three cheers for creativity, he had constructed the Witch out of balloons and covered them with brown sugar. He had then pushed a pin into the figure to produce a hollow sugar figure that would dissolve instantly when touched by the water. This would be the highlight of the whole parade! Simon was very proud of himself. He pushed his magnificent float into a large storage locker behind the palace. The room was dusty and cobwebby enough to assure him that it was not used very often and that his surprise would not be discovered before the day of the parade.

"Now I'll need to find a bucket and fill it with water," he said. Looking around the room, he noticed an oak bucket that was already full and which was just the right size for his sculpture. He quickly secured it in place in the papier maché Dorothy's hands. "If this doesn't get a lot of loud cheers from the crowd, nothing will!" He rubbed his paws with glee.

CHAPTER FOUR
AN UNFORTUNATE OUTCOME

The day of the big parade came swiftly. Sir Simon and Kabumpo were vastly proud of the surprise they were about to spring on the people of the Emerald City. Indeed, it was a delightful parade. The Fuzzy Yellow Wogglebugs had put together a choral group that sang a bouncing tune as they marched at the head of the parade. Mr. Tinker followed them with an electronic float that tossed candy canes out of its windows to the people below. Princess Saari came next, riding atop a magnificent float that seemed to radiate all the colors of the rainbow. She was followed by Pegina the Pegasus, who flew just above the heads of two mighty dragons. Button-Bright, Trot, and Betsy Bobbin had put together a kazoo band and played "Ease on Down the Road" as they marched along behind the dragons. The Elves of Elfland followed, having constructed a float that resembled Egor's fantastic Funhouse out of hundreds of carnations. A gray spotlight shot out of the windows at certain intervals to circle around the Funhouse and resemble a cyclone. No one knew how the Elves had managed to make the light do this trick, but it was an Elven secret, so no one asked.

Many other quaint and delightful spectacles were there to be seen and enjoyed. But it was the marvelous Dorothy and Wicked Witch sculpture that caught the attention of everyone. It reminded all of the reason for the annual celebration, and all were happy to recall the way they had been freed from the heartless whims of the cruel-hearted old woman.

At the end of the parade, all eyes were fixed on the image, and Simon signaled to Kabumpo to let go of the spring. The Dorothy statue splashed the sugary Witch right on her head. Unfortunately, the bucket had not been filled with water, as Simon had assumed. It was actually filled with some fermented sucopinesz juice that a family of wombats had hidden there for consumption after the parade. The Witch image began to shrink and fall away. The crowd roared and laughed at the sight. But, of course, we all know that sucopinesz juice and sugar do not mix well. A series of tiny explosions began to appear above the melted Witch. Kabumpo was so startled that he did not see how close he was getting to the Hungry Tiger. Feeling a heavy elephant's foot on his striped tail, the Tiger jumped eight hundred yards ahead. He landed on Princess Saari, breaking a hole in the top of her float, into which they both fell. From this hole emanated a radiant green light. The light ricocheted off of the Glass Cat's tail and struck the gray light that had been circling the Elfland float. Now, it is commonly known among Oz scholars that a cyclone is created when hot and cold air meet in one place. It was the same way when the two magical types of light collided. The dizzying green light splashed at the other-worldly gray light, and a funnel cloud emerged. It whirled about until it surrounded the popping mass of sugared juice. When the twister had subsided, thanks to the magic of Glinda and the Wizard, there stood a hideous green-faced woman in a black outfit. On her head she wore a black pointed hat. In her hand was a broomstick.

"Who's sh-she?" stuttered Dorothy.

"I don't know," replied Ozma. "She looks like a Witch! But not like any of the Witches I've ever known about!"

"I am the Wicked Witch of the West!" shouted the woman in a maniacal voice.

"She doesn't look like the one I remember," said the Scarecrow. "This one has two eyes and green skin. She must be an impostor."

"I am not an impostor!" bellowed the woman.

"But," said an elderly Winkie who remembered the original Witch, "Witch Allidap had a patch over one eye and did not dress in pure black. This is not her at all."

"I am too me! I just feel a little different today, that's all. I will prove to you that I am Allidap!"

CHAPTER FIVE
THE BEST LAID PLANS

It should be understood that, although the creature was really little more than an unstable life-form produced by a one-of-a-kind series of accidents, she believed that she was indeed the Wicked Witch of the West. And as long as she suffered under this delusion, she was dangerous to all of the Witch's enemies. Especially Dorothy, as her primary memory was based upon the scene on the float, rather than any history before or after the event depicted thereon. She was angry and afraid, these being the emotions that were depicted in the sculpture. And these emotions, as we all know, can lead one to do things that are not particularly wholesome. Now, it was not too many seconds before the false Witch hopped onto her broomstick and zoomed away from the jeering crowd. She was a creature of resentment and hate, so she did not feel safe in that environment. Instead, she determined to find a way to reach her goals elsewhere. Knowing about the castle where the real Witch had lived, she hid herself there to get her bearings. Because she was not really Witch Allidap, she did not know much magic. But, because of the magic in the colored lights, she knew just enough to keep her from realizing the truth about her identity. Her appearance was quite different from that of the real Allidap. There was a reason for this, however. It seems that, at the very millisecond of her being brought to life, someone who believed in her had thought about her. And that someone had had a different impression of her. It was a silly impression created not so much by the book as by a movie musical that was televised annually. So that was the way the thinker imagined her to look. Because of this, he had projected his impression onto the false Witch. It also created a number of Allidap's memories in the mind of the sugar-creature. And it also caused her to remember the thinker—a little boy named Graham. He had been thinking about the original book but visualized the Witch as she had looked in the movie. And because he had an inordinate amount of homework to do, he was also feeling quite resentful. Little did he dream that this combination of negative emotions and vivid imagination would bring into manifestation a very unpleasant creature! One that no decent young person should ever have to encounter. But now Graham found himself face to face with the Wicked Witch!

She was in his home, and she was hardly filled with joy. She dragged him to her castle and laughed at his utter helplessness. "You're just afraid of what I might do to you," she said. "Look at you. You're shaking in your boots!"

"I am afraid, yes," said Graham. "Really afraid. But I don't think you'll harm me after you hear what I have to say."

"Oh," replied the Witch. "Really? And what might that be?"

"Listen carefully," said Graham. "I know where there is a book of magic spells that can make mincemeat out of Dorothy and the Scarecrow and those guys."

"You do?" the Witch said, skeptically. "And what is a book?"

"Why, it is a bunch of pieces of paper stuck together at one side and that has words printed inside of it."

"Oh, yes," said the Witch. "I know what words are. I had some words of warning printed on some signposts to keep away strangers. And I once wrote 'SURRENDER DOROTHY' in the sky. But my memory doesn't include a book. Where is it?"

"Only I can get it," said Graham, realizing that he now had a perfect way out of the dilemma. "It is back at my home in America." (He was sure that he could break away from her once he was back home.) But not to be outsmarted, clutching the boy by the hand, the Witch immediately pulled him back through the mirror without letting him free from her vise-like grasp. "Where is this book?" she said angrily. Then, seeing Graham's math book on the table, she felt a tinge of recognition. There had been some of these on a table in her castle when she had demanded that Dorothy give her those magic shoes. So these were called books! "Is this the one?" she asked, picking up his math book with her free hand. "What are these words on it?"

"What's wrong?" asked Graham. "Can't you see? Don't your eyes work?"

"I do not know these words," said the Witch. "My memory has become clouded on some things. I know the words 'SURRENDER DOROTHY' and the ones I had on my signposts, but these are unfamiliar. What do they say?"

"It says," Graham lied, *"The Best and Most Complete Book of Witchcraft Ever Written.* It has every spell ever invented in it! Would you like to have it? If you go away, I'll give it to you."

"I'll take it, but I'll need a reader to read it to me. That shall be you, my little FOOL!" So saying, she took him back through the mirror, sealing off the opening behind them forever.

CHAPTER SIX
SPELLBOUND!

Once back on the other side of the mirror and in her own domain, the Witch could not wait to get started on the first spell. After all, who could resist experimenting with spells from a book with a title like *The Best and Most Complete Book of Witchcraft Ever Written*?

"Okay, you little squirt," she snapped. "Read me the first spell."

Graham knew he would have to think off the top of his head and think fast if he was to come up with something plausible. The minute she found out that the book was a fake, he would be dead meat, that was for sure.

"Okay. Well…. Let's see…. The first spiel—I mean, spell—is 'How to Turn an Obnoxious Dial (or Socially Disadvantaged Countenance) into a Reflection of Infinite Beauty.'"

"I haven't the faintest idea what you just said," snapped the Witch with obvious annoyance. "Read it to me again. Wait. That won't do any good. What do you think it means?"

Graham knew he had her hooked. "It is obviously a spell that will transform you into the most beautiful creature to ever walk the face of the earth."

"Oh, my," said the Witch-clone with obvious delight. "Well, let's get started! What are you waiting for?"

Graham cleared his throat and began to "read" from the book:

> "*Find a slimy little pickle. Rub it with a shiny nickel. Drop it in a Witch's hat. Add seventeen eggs on top of that. Top that off with a bowl of Jell-O and spittle from a little fellow. Add some sour cream and chives and honey directly from the hives.*
>
> *Now add one pint of strawberry jam (preferably bought from Knott's Berry Farm). Then bend thy head towards thy legs and press said hat upon thy head. Now stand and then induce a friend to pull it down below thy crown.*

"Oh, that does sound absolutely divine!" cried the Witch. "Quick! Help me gather the materials together so we can start immediately."

Graham could hardly contain himself with the thought of the true results of this experiment. And although he was going to use this opportunity to escape, he almost wished he could stay to see the whole thing through. He congratulated himself on his ability to create such an authentic-sounding spell and for having the presence of mind to suggest the half-hour lead time he would need in order to escape from the castle. When everything was ready, Graham followed the spell to the letter. And since he was the only little fellow around, he was the obvious choice to provide the spittle for the concoction—which he did with great delight.

As soon as he got to the part where he had to pull the Witch's hat down over her head, he said, "I'll keep my eye on the clock and let you know when the half hour is up." With that, he jammed the hat down over her eyes and down to her shoulders and then made a beeline for the window.

CHAPTER SEVEN
AN ALIEN PRESENCE

After Graham had escaped from the castle, he thought about the Witch standing there for a full half-hour and thinking how beautiful she was going to be when she took the hat off and looked at herself in her mirror. He laughed out loud as he imagined how she would really look with that gooey mess all over her hair and face and clothes. But he knew that once the reality dawned on her that the spell was a fake, that she was just as ugly as ever, and that he had escaped, she would be absolutely beside herself with rage. The boy's elation began to change to fear as he considered the possible repercussions of his actions. Here he was in a strange yellow land with no idea of where he was going or where to hide.

He had been traveling through a wooded area which, for now, offered some measure of security, since he would be hidden from aerial surveillance, when he came upon a clearing. Actually, it was more than just a clearing; it was a perfectly round grassy clearing about fifty feet in diameter, and dome-shaped. As he studied the dome, it began to slowly rise, exposing a round house with windows and doors and a grass-covered roof. Graham stood perfectly still, waiting to see if anyone came out. When it was obvious that no one was coming, he cautiously walked toward the house to see if he could see through the window. Suddenly, a loud, mechanical-sounding voice filled the air. "WARNING! YOU ARE APPROACHING TOO CLOSE TO THE VEHICLE. PLEASE STEP BACK."

At this point, Graham was more than a little confused. He knew that this sort of proximity alarm system was favored by some motor vehicle owners back home. But the device seemed very out of place in Oz. Not to mention the fact that the sound was emanating from a house, not a car. At that moment, the round roof slowly started to spin and rose about four feet above the house and hovered there. The outside walls receded back into the ground to reveal a bright, shiny spaceship shimmering in the sunlight. A ramp unfolded to reveal two equally shimmering space beings. They descended (or rather, floated) down the ramp and stopped less than three feet from the boy. They were not very tall—about four feet in height—and they were dressed in metallic-looking one-piece spacesuits that closely followed the contour of their slender bodies. They had quite large heads, which were somewhat out of proportion to their overall physique. Their eyes were large and doe-shaped and were the blackest of black with no pupils visible. He sensed an intelligence emanating from their eyes that was far in excess of ordinary people. Their skin was of a dull grayish hue; no color at all.

Graham waited for them to speak (for some reason he was totally unafraid). One of them raised his right hand in greeting. He spoke without moving his lips. At least, Graham heard the words clearly inside his head but could sense no outside sound.

"Greetings, young friend. You stumbled upon our location, but it is of no consequence. We know that you bear us no ill will."

"Indeed not," replied Graham. "In fact, I am honored to make your acquaintance. I've always wanted to meet a space person."

"Well," replied the other being, "you are a space person, too."

"I am?" said Graham incredulously. "I'm afraid you're mistaken … I am from earth."

"And where, my little friend, do you think earth is? Is it not suspended in space like all of the other planets? And does it not make a complete rotation upon its axis every twenty-three hours, fifty-six minutes and four point zero-nine seconds, and at a speed of a thousand miles per hour? And does it not orbit your sun every three hundred and sixty-five days and six hours and nine minutes and nine point five seconds, and at a speed of about twenty miles per second? And does it not revolve along with the moon, around a common center of gravity, and move with the entire solar system through your local star system at thirteen miles per second? And does not your local star system move within the Milky Way at the rate of two hundred miles per second, and does not the Milky Way drift with respect to the remote external galaxies at the rate of one hundred miles per second and in all different directions, and does not your galaxy itself make a complete rotation about an axis every two hundred million years? And does it not travel through space with over a hundred billion other suns of its galactic family, not to mention an untold number of other planets?"

Graham nodded meekly. "I knew our planet was in space. I just didn't know all the details."

"Well," continued the being, "even if you mortals could travel at the speed of light, it would still take you a hundred thousand years to cross your galaxy from edge to edge."

The spaceman motioned toward the craft. "However, our ship could visit the Andromeda galaxy, which is about two million one hundred thousand light years from earth, and return before you could say *Stephen Hawking.* I'd say that is a little bit faster than the speed of light. We could not afford to waste two million years—actually, over four million years round trip! We'd never get anything done."

"Now, wait just a minute," said Graham. "You can't go faster than the speed of light. They told us in school that would be against the laws of physics!"

"We learned long ago," replied the spaceman, "that the laws of physics kept us very tightly bound until we found we could gain dominion over those laws. You see, we earned that right over a long period of time. Dominion over physical law requires a certain knowledge of science beyond the physical as well as a working knowledge of the spiritual laws. The two must work hand in hand. For example, your scientists are working strictly from a physical perspective. They are totally unaware that the atoms—the building blocks of matter—have a counterpart of a higher frequency: one that falls outside of the realm of what you would term physical. In any event, without that counterpart the physical world as you know it could not exist.

"Now, I want to demonstrate to you the practical aspects of our knowledge. Our spaceship is vibrating at the atomic rate of the collective atoms that comprise the material makeup of said ship. Now, as we observe the ship, I am going to concentrate on this counterpart of the atom that your scientists might refer to as antimatter or antiparticle. These antiparticles are what we would call the pure state of the atom. You might say they are the inner core of the atom. You might even say that they are the very soul of the atom, since they furnish the power that maintains the motion of the atom. In any event, this is the medium we work with. Incidentally, if you could observe the motion of this counterpart to the atom, you would see that it is in constant motion as it conveys its power to the atom. It turns incessantly upon its own axis, spinning like a top. It is constantly pulsating, gyrating, and, I might even say, dancing in a most beautiful manner.... I might tell you at this point that the name we give to this wonderful animating force, is, quite naturally, the anim. Now I am going to concentrate on the atomic structure of our ship. I am going to raise the rate of vibration, or frequency, of the individual atoms to the higher rate of the anim state. As I do so, the ship will no longer be detected by your eye-to-brain circuits. To your limited senses it will be completely invisible to you. It is this little trick that plays havoc with the minds of your fellow mortals that occasionally catch a glimpse of our ships in your skies, only to see them disappear in an instant.

Now, as I continue to concentrate, I am projecting the ship to a certain coordinate: namely, a specific planetary member of the galaxy Andromeda. This is done at the speed of thought, which is instantaneous. There…." The starship vanished in less than a blink. "Now it's back again!" the spaceman announced. And, indeed, it truly was! "Well, what do you think?"

Of course, Graham was beside himself. He could not speak. "Wow!" he said eventually. "Wow!"

"Naturally," continued the spaceman, "I had to lower the vibrations again to re-manifest it into your reality. But it is this manner of transportation that enables us to come and go as we please and, in doing so, somewhat confuse your scientists and governmental authorities."

Graham smiled.

"Speaking of your scientists," added the other alien, "they would probably be very interested to know that, long before the countless solar systems were brought into manifestation—in reference to the many planets, stars, gaseous bodies, and so forth—space was null and void of all that is now in existence. The theater of infinite space was empty. The actors had not yet made their appearance. Everything, every solitary atom (and that includes the atoms that presently constitute your body and mine), were back in that great Core of Life. The Oneness. The Source of All. Some like to call this presence God. It is, however, a presence that is very real, even to scientists who call themselves agnostics. If it were possible to become attuned to this presence, this Core of Life, you would be aware of pulsating with it. You would realize that you are receiving a great force which enables you to move about in your physical body. This force is constantly nourishing every atom that is out there in space, every atom within the earth. It is the great unifying force that your scientists suspect must exist but have never quite been able to get a handle on. However, they are getting closer to it with the discovery of so-called dark matter. But to continue: the Core of Life may be pictured as a great sun, and yet this would not describe it, for it is larger than any sun could ever possibly be. And if we were to try to measure it—and there would be no way to do this—we would find that it would encircle not only one solar system, but many other solar systems beyond. However, I am digressing from my story of the creation of the universe. Gradually or suddenly, depending on your viewpoint in the great consciousness of time, the animatical forces from the Core of Life caused the great expansion from the etheric state of matter, causing gross material to manifest through friction and be slushed off and begin to solidify. And when it did, the planets began to form. First one began to form over here, and then another one began to form over there, and these in turn were followed by still others until gradually, within the great power that is concentrated at the point where the planets were revolving, a great solar system came into manifestation. Then, after their birth, the planets were dormant for what may have been many millions of years while they were going through the cooling process. Then, gradually, over perhaps many million more years, the germinal kingdom brought forth the different forms of matter, bacteria, et cetera. These in turn brought forth the various bodies, the animalistic kingdom, and other forms of life that would be needed to help build and prepare the way and become an assisting force in eventually bringing forth the human expression. So you see, it was all carefully orchestrated by that driving presence I mentioned. We are now living in the seventh group of planets. Yes, the universe as you know it existed in six previous manifestations, returning each time to its original state. This seventh manifestation is the last. The time will come when there will be no physical planets, no physical remnants of this present universe. But not to worry, my little friend. You and I and, indeed, all expressions of what you might refer to as life will continue on, for life is eternal. It has always existed, and it always will exist. The physical expression is only a temporary condition. By the way, in our haste we forgot to introduce ourselves. My name is Agasha, and my brother here is Araskus. Your world will, no doubt, be reading more about us. As a matter of fact, as we speak, I am receiving a telepathic message from a William Eisen who now resides in Oz. He reminds me that while in America he brought forth some of my philosophy in written documents entitled *Agasha: Master of Wisdom* and *The Agashan Discourses*. These works were written for adults, but older children who have an advanced understanding may appreciate them, too. Mr. Eisen was a personal friend of Mr. Evans, who at this moment is recording these very events as they occur."

The two beings then shook hands with the boy and bid him farewell as they returned to their ship. Moments later, the craft arose and tilted in salute as it spun away beyond the horizon. Graham stood for the longest time, staring at the spot where the spaceship had disappeared from sight. There were so many more questions he wanted to ask, and he wondered if he would ever again have the opportunity. One question he meant to ask was that if it took two million, three hundred thousand some years for light to reach Earth from the Andromeda galaxy, would that mean that we would be observing it as it existed two point three million years ago? And that if it suddenly disappeared at this moment in our time, would we not know it for another two point three million years? That seemed like a very good question to ask, for it would mean that when we look out into space, we are really looking back into time. Now that he thought of it, his science teacher had said that it takes eight minutes for light to reach us from the sun, so, if the sun disappeared three minutes ago, we would not know it for another five minutes. What a thought! Graham realized that not a solitary soul back home would ever believe one word of his communication with the space people, assuming, that is, that he would ever be foolish enough to try to tell anyone. But the first thing he would try to do would be to find the books Agasha had mentioned. He would do this the minute he got home…

HOME! OH MY GOSH! HOW LONG HAD HE BEEN GONE? AND HOW WAS HE GOING TO GET BACK? WHY, OH WHY HAD HE NOT TRIED TO HITCH A RIDE WITH THE SPACE PEOPLE?

CHAPTER EIGHT
A STRANGE ENCOUNTER

Graham mentally kicked himself for not thinking of asking the UFO people for a ride back to America. He had felt so much in awe of the magnificent spaceship and its unique occupants, though, that it had never entered his mind to ask a selfish favor of them. He now regretted that feeling. After all, the two aliens had made it obvious that they meant to serve him and help him to learn. Surely they would never have considered it a selfish request on Graham's part had he simply asked that they drop him off in America on their way to wherever they might have been headed. But it was, alas, a little bit too late to cry over spilled milk. Instead, Graham had far more important matters to attend to. He had, after all, come into a very strange land where the physical laws he was used to no longer seemed to apply. Not only that, but his presence would be missed before too long, and he did not want to cause undue worry back home. But even more immediate: he had a powerful and very wicked Witch to deal with who would soon catch on to his lies, and she was not going to be at all happy with him. Had Graham been a lesser boy, he might have broken down and cried. But Graham decided instead to make the most of the grave situation. He continued to walk past the area where the UFOlanders had been. His main concern now was to get as far away as possible from the awful old Witch's castle. He was wondering in which specific direction to go when he heard a noise in the trees. At first he could not identify the sound, although it was a familiar sound. Because it was so far out of place in Oz, it did not register at first. But, yes! Now he was certain. It was the sound of a television set. That is to say, the sound of human voices that could only be coming from a radio or TV. It is a sound you simply cannot mistake. Now the sound was getting louder. It was coming toward him. *What on earth could a television set be doing here*? Graham thought. And how could it be moving toward him? The answer immediately became known when out from a clump of trees walked a robotic looking creature. He had triangular shaped legs and arms and body. In place of a face he had a portable television set. Not only that, but the channels kept changing. First Channel Two with the evening news. Then Channel Four with a basketball game. Then Channel Seven with *Jeopardy!*

Then Channel Eleven with a program about UFOs. Then Channel Thirteen with a commercial for Head and Shoulders anti-dandruff shampoo. And so on, and so on. Well, this was the strangest sight to behold. A walking television set. It walked right up to Graham and stopped right up against his face. Then the screen went blank for a moment and a face appeared. That is to say, not a human face exactly, but sort of a cartoon type of face with large, bushy eyebrows; big, expressive eyes; a prominent nose; and a mouth in the shape of a big grin. "Howdy doody," said the mouth as the thing's hand shot out and grabbed Graham's hand in a vigorous handshake.

"How—How—How—" stammered Graham.

"HowHowHow?" inquired the voice. "That's a funny word. I never heard it before."

"Ah … eh …" said Graham, his voice still a bit shaky. "I was actually trying to say, 'How do you do?'"

"Oh, I see," replied the being, "but how do I do what?"

"No. I mean I'm trying to say, er … 'howdy doody' to you."

"Oh. Now I understand. I'm sorry for being so dumb. But you see, my entire vocabulary comes from TV shows. I never actually went to school, so some things I do not know. I beg of you, forgive me!" he shouted as he bent down on one knee and held Graham's hand.

"There's no need to be so dramatic," said Graham. "I forgive you."

"Oh, thanks a bunch," the creature said. "Is there anything you'd like to watch? You can watch any television show that's ever been recorded in television history. Just say the word."

"Well, nothing right now," Graham answered. "But I'm really curious as to how you came into being."

"HOW! I! CAME! INTO! BEING? Hmmmmm. Oh, you mean how I was manufactured. Well, originally a tinsmith made me. But then I lost my head over a girl. Then one day an electrical genius from Mars came to Oz to discuss a contract to build satellite dishes. They wanted to bounce signals from Mars to earth in order to relay Martian soap operas in exchange for some earth programming to Mars. Their favorite earth programs are reruns of *Mork and Mindy* and *Star Trek*. They're even more popular than their prime-time blockbuster, *My Favorite Earthling.* Anyway … as I was saying … Let's see … I had lost my head, and—"

"Now, wait a minute!" Graham interrupted. "There are no people on Mars. Besides, the environment there is too hostile to support life."

"Oh. You mean that they have too many harsh TV critics?"

"No. I mean that—For one thing, the temperature would be too harsh. It's way too cold on Mars to support life. Not to mention the atmosphere, which is mostly carbon dioxide."

"Oh, my dear boy," smiled the face. "You don't know anything, do you? Oh, you know your scientific facts all right but, according to my memory banks, there is life all over the universe that your scientists' crude observation methods cannot even detect."

"You're beginning to sound like the UFO people I talked to," Graham answered with a tone of disapproval in his voice.

"Well, nevertheless, life exists simultaneously on many different frequency levels that are undetectable from one to the other—an analogy would be the many TV channels that are in the air simultaneously, but you can only tune in to the one frequency that your tuning device is locked into."

"Well, I've heard that before," answered Graham.

"Yes. And people are tuning devices in themselves. That's why some people are sensitive to the vibrations from Oz and can see what is going on there. Mr. Baum was the first person in America who was able to tune into Oz, and he wrote many history books on this land. Well, that is to say, they were recordings of current events at the time he wrote them, but they are now history. And as much as he wrote, he was only able to record a tiny fraction of our history. Since then, many people have contributed. Some more than others."

"I wonder why no one in America was able to tune into Oz before L. Frank Baum," Graham said.

"Because there are millions of frequencies, but he happened to hit the right one one day when he was telling stories to the children. He was very lucky to hit it because of the tremendous odds against him. But once he did, it was easy after that. And it was easy for other people to follow him because they knew it could be done and kept persevering until they were able to tune in themselves. The secret is not to give up if you are truly interested, because once you lock into it, you become better attuned as time goes by. I heard a good example of this sort of thing on my sports channel just the other day. They were discussing Roger Bannister and how he broke the four minute mile in 1954 and that no one in earth's history up until that time believed it could be done, so no one did it. But once Mr. Bannister ran the mile in three minutes and fifty-nine point four seconds, other people broke the record because now they knew it was possible after all. They had never really tried hard enough before that, because they simply did not believe.

This just shows that you can do anything you set your mind to do as long as you believe it's possible. Let me recite a poem I heard once on my Public Television channel. This poem, if my memory banks serve me right, is by a gentleman by the name of C.W. Longenecker:

The Victor

If you think you are beaten, you are.
If you like to win but think you can't,
Its almost a cinch you won't
If you think you'll lose, you're lost.
For out in the world we find
Success begins with a fellow's will.
It's all in the state of wind.
If you think you are outclassed, you are.
You've got to think high to rise.
You can ever win a prize.
Life's battles don't always go
To the stronger or faster man.
But sooner or later, the man who wins.
Is the one who thinks he can."

"That's very inspirational," said Graham. "I must remember that. But doesn't it apply equally to girls?"

"Oh, of course!" the TV responded. "But the poem was written a long time ago, before non-specific gender language was in vogue."

"You seem rather wise for a manufactured person," said Graham. "Where did your brain come from?"

"Oh, I haven't really got a brain in the traditional sense of the word. My brain is largely electronic and preprogrammed from a lot of things I've seen and heard on TV. There are lessons to be learned, even from the poorest of shows."

"Do you have a name?" asked Graham.

"Well, most of my friends call me Telle. My full name is Telle Visionary. But you can just call me Telly."

CHAPTER NINE
CAPTURED AGAIN!

"Well, Telly, you are a most fascinating person. Would you like to accompany me on my mission? You see, I am a stranger in a strange land, and I'd feel a lot better with someone like yourself who is familiar with the way things work here. Also, I haven't the slightest idea where I am or where I'm going. Not only that, but I escaped from a Wicked Witch and she's probably mad as heck right now and looking for me."

"I'd be delighted to accompany you, my little friend. Although I must tell you, I don't know how much protection I could give you from the Wicked Witch because, if it's the one I think it is, she's bullied me from time to time. Whenever she sees me, she zooms right in and makes me run all the soap operas she's missed. Sometimes I have to sit for hours and hours while she catches up. By the way, what is the mission you mentioned?"

"Oh, my mission is to get home to America," Graham answered quickly. "My parents must be worried sick about me. Have you any ideas how I could get back before that Witch captures me again?"

"Well, let's see! Hmmm, dum de dum de dum, Hmmm, um, let me think…"

There was a long pause. "No!" he finally said. "I can't think of a single way you could get back to America. In fact, I really don't think it's even possible for a human being to get back once he's here. The only person I know of who ever did that was Dorothy Gale of Kansas. And the reason I know that is that I run the movie every year and the end is always the same. Dorothy clicks her heels together three times and says, 'There's no place like home, there's no place like home, et cetera,' and she wakes up in her bed back in Kansas. Now, there's an idea! How about we go and see Dorothy? She'll know how to get you back. Why didn't I think of that first?"

"Wonderful!" the boy exclaimed. "I'm beginning to feel a lot better. What is Dorothy doing now? Is she—" Graham's question was cut short by a big, extremely loud popping sound and a cloud of smoke. When the smoke cleared, who should be there but the Wicked Witch, grinning from ear to ear and prancing up and down with excitement!

"Well, my little friend. Found you at last, haven't I? Loved your spell! Oh, it was terrific! See how beautiful I look? DO YOU? DO YOU?" she screamed, grabbing him by the scruff of the neck. "Look at me. Look, I say!" she yelled as she jerked his face to hers. "Do I look more beautiful to you? Let's see. What was the last line of that spell … Oh, now I remember: Look in the mirror and you shall see, none more beautiful than thee! You little liar. LIAR! Did you hear me?"

"How could I not?" asked Graham. "The way you're carrying on, I assume there are people in Kansas who can hear you." But he cowered behind Telly as he said so.

"Hello, my good woman," said Telly, holding out one of his peculiar triangle-shaped arms. His handshake was not accepted by the wicked woman. "Allow me to say that you are more exquisitely beautiful than any of the television stars I've ever seen or heard of!" said the robotic man. "And believe you me, I have run more Miss America beauty pageants than you can shake a stick at. You are lovelier than any of those girls. You are more innocently ravishing than Ginger Grant on Gilligan's Island! You are the epitome of human grace and style! You make all other women pale beside you!"

"Huh?" said the Witch, dropping Graham like a sack of potatoes. He caught his breath and tried to stand up, but the Witch had put one of her big, long feet on his chest to hold him down. "What are you talking about, Tube-face?" the Witch asked of the television-person.

"I am just admiring your gorgeousness!" said Telly in a musical tone of voice. "Are you the next TV heart-throb? The next Susan Lucci? Are you going to take the couch potatoes of the world by storm and make all of them yearn to be you? You could, you know. You surely are already the envy of everyone who has ever laid eyes upon you!"

The Witch looked at her prisoner. "What is this machine up to, boy? And you'd best not lie to me again!"

"Oh, no!" replied Graham. "I have learned my lesson, to be sure. I wouldn't think of telling another lie."

"Then what is this clinking, clanking, clattering collection of caliginous junk babbling about?" she sneered.

"I'm truly relishing your magnificent beauty!" repeated Telly.

"My friend is simply admiring your beauty, like he said," answered Graham, not sure why Telly was acting this way, but deciding it would be best to play along. "I think he is quite smitten with you!"

"Really?" said the Witch. "Tell me more."

"You are truly a vision of loveliness!" charmed Telly in a most dramatic manner. "My heartstrings are all going ZING!"

"They are?" the Witch said, somewhat perplexed. "Maybe the spell worked after all. I guess it was a delayed reaction. Give me a mirror! I want to see how I look!"

"Er… You don't want to do that," said Graham. "You… er… You are so gorgeous that no mirror could possibly capture your true image."

"That's altogether silly and utterly foolish, young man! Now that I am pretty, I want to look upon myself." The Witch took her foot off his chest and let him stand up. "Now fetch me a mirror, or I will turn mean!"

"Such beauty could never do harm to anyone," said Telly. "You are only meant to be worshipped!"

"Thank you," the Witch said. Then, realizing that she had actually said something polite, she added, "You bizarre jumble of soup cans and gigabytes."

She saw that Graham had made no move to obtain a mirror, so she pushed him over again. "Okay, slime-twirp. I'll get my own mirror!" She switched off Telly's picture in order to catch her reflection in the blank screen. Telly, thinking quickly, distracted her for a moment and switched the screen back on while at the same time calling up an image of Eva Gabor from his archives.

When Graham saw what had happened, he held his teeth tightly together and clenched his fists in anxiety. How would the crone react?

"My … My … My goodness!" she said. "I really am something, aren't I?" She smiled a hideous grin. "Just looky there! I am beautiful!"

Graham's anxiety quickly subsided. Telly's clever ploy had worked. "You are a vision of loveliness," said the boy.

"I am, aren't I? I'm gorgeous!" She then began to dance and flitted around like a young girl as she broke into a rendering of a song from the musical play *West Side Story*:

"I feel pretty … Oh so pretty
I feel pretty and witty and gay
And I pity
Any girl who isn't me today
I feel charming
Oh so charming

It's alarming how charming I feel
And so pretty
That I hardly can believe I'm real!"

After she finished the song, she closed her eyes in sheer ecstasy and heaved a long, contented sigh. She stood there like that for the longest time. Graham and Telly quickly seized the moment and tiptoed behind a hedgerow and, as soon as they were out of earshot, they ran like the wind as far as they could go. As soon as they felt they were safe, they collapsed in a heap in uncontrollable laughter.

CHAPTER TEN
A MYSTICAL EXPERIENCE

It had been quite some time since escaping from the Witch again, and the two friends walked along the road lost in thought. Well, that is to say, Graham was lost in thought, whereas Telly was absent-mindedly playing an old commercial:

> *Double your pleasure, double your fun, Get double ev'rything*
> *rolled into one, Oh, double your pleasure, double your fun, with*
> *double good, double good, Double-mint gum.*

Suddenly, the pair came across a sign at the side of the road which read:

OZ INTERNATIONAL AIRPORT DEPARTURES UPPER LEVEL ARRIVALS LOWER LEVEL FOLLOW THE BLUE SIGNS FOR THE UPPER LEVEL FOLLOW THE RED SIGNS FOR THE LOWER LEVEL

"Telly!" cried Graham. "Telly! I can't believe it! An airport in Oz? Why didn't you tell me? Now I can go home. All I have to do is buy a ticket. They can call my dad and get his credit card number."

"Now wait a minute!" Telly exclaimed. "Not so fast, my young friend. There is no airport in Oz. Never was, and never will be. It's just not possible for airplanes to fly here from anywhere. Queen Ozma herself saw to that after a certain incident with a little girl and a pet monkey. No, this cannot be for real. Must be some kind of trick."

Graham was crestfallen. He was just not prepared to accept such a dismal opinion. "Oh, no! I'm sure you're mistaken. They wouldn't have a sign like that if there was no airport there."

"Well, I hate to say I told you so. But you'll see when we get there that there's nothing there," Telly said emphatically. "At least, not an airport …" He suddenly stopped in his tracks. "I can't believe what I'm seeing!" he shouted incredulously as the sight of a huge airport (the size of L.A. International) loomed up ahead.

"SEE! I told you so!" shouted Graham with obvious delight as he ran forward. "Home sweet home, here I come!"

"Not so fast!" warned Telly. "Not so fast! It has to be a trick. Maybe the Wicked Witch has created an illusion and … and it's really her castle…."

But Graham was already out of earshot. Before him loomed a giant 747 glistening in the sun, its huge jet engines screaming with impatience for full power to be applied, and the passenger door was open at the top of the stairs with a smiling flight attendant beckoning Graham aboard. "Hurry up!" she called. "We're ready to take off, and you're running late."

Graham scurried up the stairs as fast as his little legs would carry him…. The flight attendant checked his name off a list, and the door closed quickly, leaving Graham with no time to say goodbye to Telly, who was at that moment looking up at the plane forlornly as it taxied forward toward the runway. Meanwhile, Graham was being bundled into his seat and buckled into his seatbelt by the pretty flight attendant. It was only then that he remembered that he had not purchased a ticket, nor had he had a chance to say goodbye to Telly. He was seated alone by the window and quickly looked out to see if he could catch a glimpse of his friend. But it was too late; the plane was already at the end of the runway and several feet into the air with the countryside whizzing past and getting smaller and smaller as the plane quickly ascended.

The captain's voice came over the intercom loud and clear. "Good morning, ladies and gentlemen. This is your captain speaking. We have departed Oz International Airport and will be cruising at twenty thousand feet. We should be arriving at our destination in about three hours. You may remove your seatbelts and make yourselves comfortable. Refreshments will be served shortly, and you may watch our in-flight movie if you wish."

Graham looked around to see who else was sharing his flight. He was astonished to see that there were no other passengers at all. Now he began to get frightened. Why would a great big airplane take off with no passengers except himself? And who was that captain addressing when he said "ladies and gentlemen"? He was beginning to feel that he had been caught up in an episode of Telly's *Twilight Zone*. Just then, he caught a glimpse of a portly gentleman approaching him from the front of the plane. He assumed there was another passenger after all, one who must have been sitting in the front seat, and too low for his head to be visible. However, as the gentleman approached closer to where Graham was seated, the boy became even more perplexed. The gentleman in question was none other than William Shakespeare! Oh, there was no mistaking such an historical figure. Graham had seen paintings and drawings of him many times. And his clothes and features were an exact replica of those portrayals. Not only that, but he was carrying a great big book entitled *The Complete Works of William Shakespeare*.

Suddenly Graham flushed with embarrassment. How could he think for one moment that this was William Shakespeare? The fellow was obviously an actor, perhaps on his way home from making a movie and so late for his flight that he did not have time to change his clothes or remove his makeup. At that moment the gentleman spoke … "Good day, my dear fellow. My name is William Shakespeare. Do you mind if I sit here? The plane's rather crowded and I see that you have the whole aisle to yourself."

"Okay! That's it," thought Graham. "The guy's a definite nut case. Must have escaped from the looney bin and somehow got to Oz. The plane's crowded indeed! He and I are the only passengers! Every single seat is empty." However, "Mr. Shakespeare" seated himself next to Graham without waiting for a reply. "I know that you don't believe I'm who I say I am," he said. "But I can assure you, I am he who is often referred to as The Bard of Avon. All I'd like you to do is to tell earth's disbelievers who don't accept that I wrote my works that I did indeed write them." Without waiting for Graham to respond, he then proceeded to break into verse in a gentle, melodic voice:

"_I am he who wrote my verse,
My dramas, sonnets, quibbles, rhyme,
I'm Shakespeare still—dear England's Bard—
And shall ever be, throughout time.

I wrote, 'tis true, some sonnets, plays,
To make a living, pass the time
In merriment or jest and glee—
I turned out many a ribaled rhyme.

To set the world right,
And make snivelers agree
As to who wrote Shakespeare,
If 'twere BACON or He,

Or Marlowe or Pitt,
Or scribes ages old,
I say to them all—
The truth is now told.

When a man among kings (I was knighted by one)
Where a handle or wheel makes a favorite son
Distinguished through time for something he's done,
For a knight in his day must his laurels have won.

With a band of king's players by Bill Shakespeare led,
I played many roles, e'en recalled the dead

To piece out my plot or to string out my rhyme,
 Nor considered it theft, more an honor that time,
 To borrow a plot for a queen or a king,
 And watch their amuse as my poor muse would sing.
 So each time I needed a plot or a play
 I searched o'er the tomes where musty plots lay
 Bulging out with ideas from craniums dust,
 Whose shades may have helped as I now know and trust.
 But that any one man made a plot or a play,
 Or was such singled out as a ruse for my pay,
 I deny in *fac toto* in spirit this day.
 Should any man's play be found in my work,
 Which was not by me writ, 'tis a publisher's quirk;
 Which one day I'll acclaim; for I mean to read all
 As signed with my name_."

Young Graham was beyond words at this outpouring of verse. The mode of language was not something he could identify with in his everyday world, and it was quite beyond his level of comprehension. But he sensed this was no ordinary man in his presence. "Are you really William Shakespeare?" he ventured forth timidly. "And if you truly are, how could you still be alive hundreds of years after you were born?"

"Well, young one," smiled the Bard kindly, "that is a long story... Suffice to say I am here with you having this conversation. And look around you—many of the other passengers are people from your history books. We are en route to our home beyond the outer fringes of Oz. We are graduates of the University of Higher Consciousness, and we are on our way to Historicalfigureland. So much hatred exists in the world you come from, and where there is not exactly hatred per se, there is often indifference or even total apathy for the plight of others. And as if your world were not bad enough with the constant warring between nations, many individuals in so-called civilized lands feel the need to declare war on their neighbors. I am speaking of your young people killing each other for no other reason than that it has become the thing to do. What is so sad is that they totally lack remorse for their victims' pain and suffering and give not the slightest thought to the victims' families left behind in utter and complete desolation and sadness at their terrible loss. Our goal is to find a way to encourage people to reach out to one another—to care for one another. That is why we wrote our books and plays, to teach people what life be truly about."

Okay. That's it, thought Graham. *There's no doubt about the truth of what the old guy is saying regarding earth conditions. But the queer old boy is definitely off his rocker. First, there's definitely no other passengers on the plane, and ...*

"Good grief!" he exclaimed as the outlines of human forms began to appear in the other passenger seats. Gradually these forms became more solid until he realized that indeed the plane was filled with passengers, many of which were historical figures in the modes of dress of their particular times in history. First he saw Napoleon in the aisle to his immediate left. Then, next to him, Marie Antoinette. Then Mary, Queen-of-Scots, Henry the Eighth, and Alexander the Great. In the next aisle: Caesar Augustus, Mark Anthony, Cleopatra, Joan of Arc, Aristotle, and Plato. It seemed that every historical figure of note was present aboard the plane, not to mention a sprinkling of people from various walks of life, such as Marcus Aurelius, Jane Merrick, Kenneth Gage Baum, Fred Stone, Judy Garland, and Ray Powell. Of course, Graham did not know who everyone was by name, but many faces looked familiar to him.

"I'm terribly sorry," apologized Shakespeare. "I didn't realize that your eyes had not yet become sensitized to the higher vibrations of my friends. What must you have thought of me?" "Oh, nothing at all," cried Graham. "I mean, I hadn't really noticed all these people. I was so engrossed in what you were saying."

"Really?" replied the Bard with a twinkle in his eye. "I quite understand. People are always totally captivated by my words. Anyway, as I was saying, or rather, as I was about to say…"

At that moment, a head bent over the Bard's shoulder to say hello to Graham. It was none other than Mark Twain, whom Graham instantly recognized. And with him was a gentleman who introduced himself as Charles Dickens. He gave Graham a wink and shook his hand. "You're a fine young fellow. I predict that you will go far in life." Of course, Graham was speechless. It suddenly hit him that he was in the company of some of the world's greatest human beings. If he ever got back home and tried to tell people, they would be sure to lock him up and throw away the key. Mark Twain asked how things were going and assured him that, while the plane would not be able to transport him home, he felt certain that, when the time came, a way would be found which would enable him to return. "If not," Mark Twain said, "not to worry. There'd never be a dull moment in Oz!"

Oh, that's just great! thought Graham. Now there was a chance that he would not get back. But did not Shakespeare say that he wanted him to inform the world that he had written his own stuff? He would not have said that if he did not think that the boy would get home to tell the tale. *What am I saying?* thought Graham. *None of this is really happening. I'm just having the most gigantic, craziest dream anyone has ever had.*

"By the way," said Mark Twain, interrupting Graham's thoughts. "Here are a couple of letters I forgot to mail to my poet friend, Bayard Taylor. They should probably be in some collection somewhere so, if you'd take them back with you, I'd appreciate it. I said in one letter that I'd probably forget to stamp it, and I did." Twain handed Graham the letters and indicated that he did not mind the boy's reading them if he wanted to.

There I go again, thought Graham, *believing in my own dream*. In any event, he settled back in the seat and began to read the letters. However, before he could really get started, Charles Dickens interrupted him.

"As usual, this Twain fellow takes over and hogs the conversation. In the very near future, young Graham, you and I will get together, and I'll tell you some very interesting stories of my childhood. In the meantime," he said, scribbling on a piece of paper that had some kind of drawing on it, "I have autographed a sketch of Boz to take back with you. Boz was the name I used when I first embarked on my literary adventures. In case you are wondering if there is a cryptic connection between Boz and Baum and Oz, you'll have to keep wondering about that. I was born at Portsea, Portsmouth, a few minutes before midnight on the seventh of February, 1812, forty-four years before Mr. Baum was born. I came to Oz in 1870, when Mr. Baum was only fourteen years old. He was not destined to write about Oz until some thirty years later. Now, when you come back, I'll tell you some more about my early days, and I'll make sure that our friend Twain doesn't bask in his self-perceived limelight while we're having our important discussions."

"Now, you listen up, Mr. Dickens, sir," said Mark Twain with mock anger, for they were actually the best of friends. "I resent that, and I won't have you filling the boy's head with a lot of imaginary adventures and strange connections between words. Next you'll be telling him there's a link between the Land of Ev and Robert Evans—or even more ludicrous— that Frank Oz and Michael Ovitz of Hollywood have a mystical link to Oz because they have Oz in their names, or even more ludicrous, that you and Chris Dulabone have a connection because you both have the initials C.D. I mean, how far can you go with this stuff? I'm telling the boy about real things and about real life..."

Dickens just shook his head slowly and turned to Graham. "I really don't pay much attention to his rambling. Go ahead and read his boring letters before he has a kitten. I won't forget my promise to you, and we'll have a delightfully interesting time together, you'll see. And I promise you, my stories will not be imaginary. Oh, by the way, here's some of my correspondence you might wish to take back with you. One is a letter and note I sent to my American friend, Mr. Fields of Boston, and also some beverage recipes I sent to Mrs. Fields. Also an announcement of two plays I produced, one of which I acted in and—"

"You're not the only actor around here, Mr. Dickens, sir!" interrupted Twain. "I've acted in plays, too. For example, I was in *Loan of a Lover* in 1876. Your Mrs. Fields, by the way, said I was wonderful in it. And as long as you're producing letters you wrote to Mr. Fields, I'll give young Graham a copy of a letter that I wrote to Mr. Fields. So what do you think about that?"

Graham was astounded to hear these two world-famous personages fighting like children and competing for his attention. What would his history teacher and his fellow classmates think? He accepted the additional material, then settled down to begin reading as the two men continued to argue all the way back to their seats. He started with Mark Twain's letters. There were actually four letters, one of them completely in German, which Twain probably had not meant to hand him. But the boy read it anyway, no matter that he did not understand a word. It did not dawn on him that, if this was a dream, where did the German words come from if they were not in his consciousness to begin with? Below is a copy of the letters for the record, although it is suggested that the reader skim over them for now, as they are not relevant except as historical interest:

_Schloss-Hotel Heidelberg May 7, 1878 H. Albert

Lieber Herr Taylor:

Wir werden hier blieben viellicht für drie Monate, zum Schloss Hotel.

—Dies hotel steht about fünf und siebenzig Fuss Höhler als das Schloss, und commandirt ein Aussicht welcher ohne Ahnlichkeit in der Welt hat. (Sie mussen excuse auskratchens, interlineations.)

Ich habe heute gecalled on der Herr Professor Ihne, qui est die Professor von Englishen Zunge im University, to get him to recommend ein Deutchen Lehrer Für mich, welcher he did. Er sprach um mehrerer Americanischer authors, und meist güngstiger & vernügungsvoll von Ihrer; dass er knew you and Ihrer so wohl durch Ihrer geschereibungen; und wann Ich habe gesagt Ich sollen Ihr schreiben heute Nacht gewesen if nothing happened, er bitte mich Opfer sein compliments, und hoffe Ihnen will ihm besuchen wenn du Kommst an Heidelberg. Er war ein vortrefflicher and liebwürdiger & every way delightful alte gentleman. Man sagt Ich muss ein Pass (in der English, Passport,) haben to decken accidents. Däfur gefelligt Ihnen furnish me one. Meine Beschreibung ist vollenden: Geborn 1835; 5 Fuss 8 ein wenig unter, sometimes ein wenig oben; dunkel braun Haar und rhotes Moustache, full Gesicht, mit sehr hohe Oren and leicht grau practvolles strahlenden Augen und ein Verdammtes gut moral character. Handlungkeit, Author von Bücher. Ich habe das Deutche sprache gelernt und bin ein glücklicher Kind, you bet. With warmest regards & kindness remembrances from all our party to you & your wife and daughter.

Yrs sincerely, S. L. Clemens

The Königstuhl, June 10 [1878] Lieber Herrn Taylor:

(Don't know whether it ought to be Herr or Herrn). Am much obliged for the letter—it was from friend whom I have been trying to ferret out. Yes, we still live at the Schloss-Hotel, & shall doubtless continue to do so until the neighborhood of August—but I only eat and sleep there; my work-den is the second story of a little Wirthschaft which stands at the base of the tower on the summit of the Konigsstuhl. I walk up there every morning at 10, write until 3, talk the most hopeless and unimprovable German with the family 'til 5, then tramp down to the Hotel for the night. It is a schones Aussicht up there as you may remember. The exercise of climbing up there is invigorating but devilish. I have just written regrets to the Paris Literary Convention. I did hate to have to miss that entertainment, but I knew that if I went there & spent a fortnight it would take me another fortnight to get settled down into the harness again—couldn't afford that.

The Emperor is a splendid old hero! That he could survive such wounds never entered my head—yet by the news I judge he is actually recovering. It is worth something to be a Lincoln or a Kaiser Wilhelm—& it gives a man a better opinion of the world to show appreciation for such men—& what is better, love of them.—I have not seen anything of this outburst of affectionate indignation since Mr. Lincoln's assassination gave the common globe a sense of personal injury. Ich habe der Consul Smith gesehen ein Paar Wochen ago, & told him about that Pass, und er hat mir gesagt das er wurde be absent from this gegen—(something) zwei oder drei Wochen, aber wann er sollte hier wieder nachkommen, wollte er der pass geschlagen worden & snake it off to Berlin. Vielleicht hat er noch nicht zu Mannheim zuruck-kehrt.

Now as to the grammar of this language; I haven't conquered the Accusative Case yet (I began with that) & there are three more. It begins to seem to me that I have got to try to get along with the Accusative alone & leave the rest of this grammar to be tackled in the future life.

With our kindest remembrances to you & yours

Yrs sincerely, S. L. Clemens

Hotel de l'Ecu de Geneve Sept. 8/78

My dear Mr. Taylor:

I have learned the German language & forgotten it again; so I resume
English once more. I have just returned from a walking trip to Mont Blanc—
which I was intending to ascend, but was obliged to give up the idea, as I
had gone too early & there was still snow on it. I find your letter here; if you
will be so kind as to forward Slote's letter to the above address I think it will
be in time to catch me—& in any case I will make arrangements to have it
follow me. (I am going to try to enclose the necessary stamps in this, but if I
forget it—however, I won't)

We have been poking around slowly through Switzerland for a month;
a week hence we go to Venice—to Rome & other places later; & we are
booked for Munich Nov. 10 (for the winter.) One of these days I am going
to whet up my German again & take a run to Berlin, & have a talk with you
in that fine old tongue.

Yrs Ever

S. L. Clemens

No. 1a Karlstrasse,

(2e stock) Munich, Dec. 14 [1878]

My Dear Mr. Taylor:

When we were poking around Italy 3 or 4 weeks ago, I was told that you
were ill, but straightway saw it contradicted in a newspaper. Now comes
this paragraph in Galignani which not only shows that the contradiction
was erroneous, but shows how ignorant one may be in this country about
what is happening only a few hundred miles away; especially when one is
buried in work & neither talks with people or often looks in the paper. We
three folks are heartily glad to hear that you are coming happily out of it; &
we are venturing to hope that by this time you are wholly restored.

We are located for the winter,—I suppose. But the children are having
such a run of coughs & diptheria [sic], that I can't tell at what moment
Mrs. Clemens may take fright & flee to some kindlier climate. However,
I stick hard at work & make what literary hay I can while we tarry. Our
little children talk German as glibly as they do English, now, but the rest

of us are mighty poor German scholars, I can tell you. Rev. Twitchell (who was over here with me a while,) conceived a pretty correct average of my German. When I was talking, (in my native tongue,) about some rather private matters in the hearing of some Germans one day, Twitchel said, "Speak in German, Mark, — some of these people may understand English."

Many a time when teachers & dictionaries fail to unravel knotty paragraphs, we wish we could fly to you for succor; we even go so far as to believe you can read a German newspaper & understand it; & in moments of deep irritation I have been provoked into expressing the opinion that you are the only foreigner except God who can do that thing. I would not rob you of your food or clothes or your umbrella, but if I caught your German out I would take it. But I don't study any more, — I have given it up.

I & mine join in the kindest remembrances & best wishes to you & your family.

Sincerely Yours

Saml. L. Clemens

We are going to try to run over to Berlin in the spring_.

As Graham finished Mark Twain's last letter—the one to Mr. Fields, dated 1874—he noticed that the next letter from Dickens to Mr. Fields was dated 1867—seven years prior. He wondered if the two famous writers had actually crossed paths or had just known the Fields independent of one another. Either way, it was interesting to note that they were contemporaries. He had always imagined that Dickens had lived in a much earlier era than Twain. Well, to continue:

_Westminster Hotel, New York Sunday, Twenty-ninth December, 1867

My Dear Fields:

When I come to Boston for the two readings of the 6th and 7th, I shall be alone, as the Dolby must be selling elsewhere. If you and Mrs. Fields should have no other visitor, I shall be very glad indeed on that occasion to come to you. It is very likely that you may have some one come with you. Of course you will tell me so if you have, and I will then re'mbellish the Parker House.

Since I left Boston last, I have been so miserable that I have been obliged to call in a Dr. —Dr. Fordyce Barker, a very agreeable fellow. He was strongly inclined to stop the Readings altogether for some few days, but I pointed out to him how we stood committed, and how I must go on if it could be done. My great terror was yesterday's Matinee, but it went off splendidly. (A very heavy cold indeed, an irritated condition of the uvula, and a restlessly low state of the nervous system, were your friends maladies. If I had not avoided visiting, I think I should have been disabled for a week or so.)

I hear from London that the general question in society is, what will be blown up next year by the Fenians.

With love to Mrs. Fields, believe me,

Ever Affectionately yours, And hers, CHARLES DICKENS_

Following this letter to Mr. Fields was the note dated 1869 and the recipes for the brewing of pleasant beverages. Last was the program for the two plays at the Tavistock House Theatre. Graham was really looking forward to bringing all these things back with him.

As Graham got to the last line of the last letter, his eyes began to feel heavy. The whirlwind of activity since his abduction had caught up with him. Just as he was falling asleep, the sound of the captain's voice on the intercom jerked him awake. "Ladies and gentlemen, we are approaching Historicalfigureland International Airport. We hope you had an enjoyable flight and hope to see you again on Oz Airlines. Oh, and to our young guest from America, you are welcome to visit your friends here any time. But I'm sure you want to continue with your mission, and you will be glad to hear that we will be making an immediate turnaround after the disembarkation of our other passengers. I believe you were brought on board for the sole purpose of delivering some important documents back to America, but you are certainly welcome to stay as long as you wish."

At that, the plane landed with a slight bump and soon taxied to the terminal. The doors opened and everyone began to file out—many, anticipating that Graham would soon be returning, didn't engage him in conversation, but shook his hand warmly and wished him well. Mark Twain gave him a hug and said how much he had enjoyed his company. He said that Graham reminded him a lot of Tom Sawyer who, he said, currently lived down the street from him. Seeing Graham's puzzled expression, he quickly explained that any imaginary character an author dreams up is actually a person that the author has tuned into. And that an author rarely has an original thought in his head but is really very good at catching glimpses of activities (present, past or future) somewhere in creation.

As Mark Twain turned to the exit, Graham suddenly remembered a question that he had wanted to ask. "Oh, Mr. Twain," he called. "I wanted to ask how you came to use the name Mark Twain. I know your real name is Samuel Clemens...."

"Well," responded Twain, "no one has ever asked me that question before—Just kidding," he added quickly, seeing Graham's expression. "Yes, I am asked it all the time. The name was first used by an old Mississippi river pilot named Isaiah Sellers, who used to write items for the *New Orleans Picayune*, in which he told of his adventures. He signed them Mark Twain, which in the parlance of pilots is a leadsman call meaning two fathoms, or twelve feet. When I was a cub pilot, I wrote a burlesque on Captain Seller's articles and published it in a rival paper under the signature of Sargeant Fathom. Unfortunately, the captain was so hurt by the burlesque that he never wrote another article. I still feel badly about it to this day, for I would never have intentionally hurt the old gentleman's feelings. Anyway, in 1863, when I was working for the *Enterprise* in Virginia City, Nevada, I wanted a good pen name and, while I was trying to think of one, I received the news of the death of the good captain. This brought to mind the name Mark Twain, and so I adopted the name in his honor. I signed it first in a letter from Carson City to the *Enterprise* on February second, 1863. So now you know, my young friend," said Twain as he handed him an autographed photo of himself. "Something to keep for yourself, in remembrance of your visit here." He hugged Graham again and waved goodbye to the boy as he descended from the plane.

Several distinguished-looking gentlemen stopped to introduce themselves to Graham. One said his name was Ralph Waldo Emerson and another, Nathaniel Hawthorne. Yet another, Isaac Newton, who said Graham would probably become a scientist.

"Undoubtedly a physicist," said Albert Einstein.

"Oh, no," interjected Eugene O'Neill. "There's no question that he will be a writer." This last remark was overheard by Charles Lindbergh, who insisted that Graham would be a flyer. Then two deep resonant voices spoke in unison: "It is obvious that the boy is a born actor." The speakers were Lionel Barrymore and John Gilbert. But Senator Charles Sumner had the final word: "Whether he becomes an actor or not is immaterial: I can assure you that this young man's ultimate destiny is in the political arena."

After the distinguished group finished arguing about Graham's future vocation, they said that, since he seemed to be starting an autograph collection, they would be glad to add theirs to the list. Even John Dickens, father of Charles Dickens, signed the sheet. Then Emerson also handed him a note that he had written to—of all people—Mrs. Fields! "Don't mention this to Dickens or Twain," he said. "They'll just be jealous."

Turning to make sure Emerson had disembarked, Nathaniel Hawthorne winked at Graham and whispered, "Here's a little note that I, too, wrote to Mrs. Fields. Not a word now to Emmy, Dickybird, or Marky-Mark." Graham laughed out loud at the nicknames being given to Emerson, Dickens, and Twain, as well as the schoolboy-like antics being displayed by these great men. Then Edward Lear, who wrote *The Owl and the Pussycat*, also handed him a handwritten note to Mrs. Fields. Graham could not help but think what a popular lady this Mrs. Fields must have been in her day. He wished he could have known her.

Hawthorne then handed him a signed photograph, as did Isaac Newton, Charles Darwin, Thomas Alva Edison, Albert Einstein, and H. G. Wells. Even Stephan Crane and Rudyard Kipling produced photographs.

Mr. Shakespeare was the last to leave. He had gone back to his seat when Messrs. Twain and Dickens were vying for Graham's attention. He, too, hugged the boy as he said goodbye, then handed him a piece of paper. "I have written down the verses I recited to you earlier, my friend—just in case you are not able to remember them all. It is important that this be given, simply because so many people doubt my authorship. I suppose after it is published there will still be doubters, but so be it. Skeptics have always existed and, I assume, always will. Some people like to doubt the reality of certain phenomena that appears quite obvious to others. I suspect it makes them feel secure: something they no longer have to deal with. Well, good luck, my little friend. I'm sure you will find your way home. Oh, incidentally, I almost forgot. I didn't want to one-upmanship Dickens and Twain in their presence, but I was an actor too, you know—long before those two. You might also like to have my autographed sketch. You will note the difference in my spelling of my name and the later versions." He stuffed a piece of paper in Graham's shirt pocket as he exited.

As the plane's doors closed behind Shakespeare, the flight attendant brought Graham a refreshing glass of lemonade. His thoughts turned to Telly, who had been so sad at being left behind. He eagerly looked forward to seeing the little guy again.

Graham slept the entire trip back. He awoke just as the plane taxied to the terminal. And who should be waiting in exactly the same place as he left him but Telly, who was so glad that Graham had returned that he ran up and hugged him for the longest time.

"I knew you'd come back," he said. "That's why I waited. I knew that the plane couldn't be going to America. In fact, I still don't believe that there was any plane or airport or anything. I think it was all some trick of the Witch to confuse us. Planes simply cannot exist in Oz. Transportation is either by foot or via some magical contrivance such as the animated Gump or the famous Red Wagon."

"Well, I hate to disappoint you," replied Graham, waving the bundle of letters, photographs, and drawings in his hand. "But where do you think these came from if the whole thing was some kind of hallucination? And how could I read German words if the words weren't in my consciousness to begin with? And I certainly couldn't have made up Shakespeare's words."

"And I hate to disappoint YOU," answered Telly, quite tartly, "but you might wish to look behind you."

Graham turned to look behind him to catch a glimpse of the entire airport fading away. Not only that, but the papers in his hand had also faded away to absolute nothingness. "Oh, no!" cried the boy. "Now I have no proof of my experience!"

"That's because it never happened," Telly replied dryly.

CHAPTER ELEVEN
THE WINKIE COUNTRY

Oz was as unlike America as it could be, yet also familiar. It was not very long at all before Graham began to feel almost at home among the soft yellow countryside of the vast Winkie territory in which the pair now found themselves. In fact, Graham had come to feel so comfortable that he had all but forgotten about the evil Witch. He might have remained content and carefree indefinitely, had he not heard the growl that came forth from a nearby top-hat bush. It was a most deafening growl that sounded as terrible as a buzz-saw and as alive as an unfed zoo animal. Graham shuddered. He wondered what sort of macabre being could possibly make such a horrendous noise. Then a voice rang out. It was not a human voice at all, and this made Graham shudder even more, whereas Telly seemed quite unfazed. (That was only because he was walking and napping at the same time.) Apparently he had switched to automatic pilot, then closed his eyes as he drifted into a state of oblivion.

"Do you remember how the Wicked Witches sent the terrible Forest Monster after the Wizard?" said the voice.

"Of course I do," answered a second voice, equally unhuman-sounding "And who could forget the time Allidap sent forth those fearsome gray wolves after little Dorothy? They could easily have ripped her to shreds."

Both of the voices sounded distinctly throaty and animalistic. In fact, they sounded as a wild beast might sound, could a wild beast speak English. It occurred to Graham that this was Oz. Wild animals COULD speak English!

"And do you think that Witch pulled a good scare when she sent those angry birds to attack Dorothy and her friends?" said one of the wild creatures.

Graham could take no more of this. It was obvious that they were surrounded by hidden animals sent by the Wicked Witch to eat them (at least him; he doubted they would attempt to eat Telly, since he would be highly indigestible). He quickly jabbed Telly in his rib-cage to awaken him to the imminent danger and, at the same time, he stooped over to grab a yellow rock from the ground. It was not much of a weapon, but it would have to do. He held up the rock threateningly.

"Okay, wolves or monsters or whatever you are!" he shouted. "I hear you conspiring. And I know that you are working for the Wicked Witch! We're not going to give up without a fight, so I suggest that you all go away!" He smiled with a hint of pride in his brave speech. But suddenly, there was a rustle of leaves behind him, and a huge creature sprang out from behind a bush and leaped at the pair. Graham, not wanting to be attacked from behind, swung himself around to face the creature. As he did so, he absently lowered his weapon at the sight of two rows of gleaming white fangs and claws that could easily have torn a little boy like himself apart in an instant. He realized that the rock in his hand was a puny weapon indeed for confronting such a ferocious beast. But nevertheless, he raised it again as a sort of reflex action and thrust it directly at the teeth of the creature. At that moment, out of the corner of his eyes, he caught a glimpse of another set of jagged teeth and claws attacking from his right. It raised a huge paw and knocked him off balance. The rock fell to the ground, out of reach. The little boy watched in horror as one of the two animals stepped forward and looked at his face. The other one was watching Telly.

"What do you think?" asked one of them.

"Looks like a little boy and a tin can with arms and legs carrying a TV set," said the other.

"The boy's not all dressed in yellow, so he's not a Winkie."

"Nor is he all in blue, like a Munchkin."

"Or purple, red, or green. He matches none of the Oz colors. I wonder where he came from."

"Maybe he's from Ev. Or Ix."

"Can you speak, boy?"

Graham struggled to sit up, while Telly just stood and glared at the beasts. He was not happy with their description of him and was seriously considering giving them a tongue-lashing, but thought discretion was the better part of valor, at least for the moment.

When Graham was able to collect himself, he discovered that the two beasts walked on all fours and were of the feline persuasion. These were no hungry wolves or monsters at all. Actually, they were a lion and a tiger.

As Graham jumped to his feet, the lion sprang backward. "Yikes!" he screamed, jumping behind the tiger. "Is he g-going to h-hurt us?"

"I don't think so," answered the tiger. "I imagine he's just getting up to look for some din-din." At this point, as if on cue, a loud growl echoed from the vicinity of the tiger. Not from his mouth or throat, but from the deepest recesses of his tummy.

Graham looked at Telly, and Telly looked at Graham.

"Apparently," said Graham, "the angry growling that we heard was nothing more than the sounds of an empty stomach. So you aren't slaves of the bad Witch, or sent to kill me?"

The tiger looked a little sheepish, which is not easy for a tiger to do.

"Of course not," he said. "Don't you know who I am? I am the Hungry Tiger of Oz. Everyone's heard of me. There have been volumes of books written about me! I am always hungry, but I am not a carnivore. I am afraid I would feel just awful if ever I ate up one of my fellow beings. Here in the Land of Oz, as you know, all creatures are treated equally. I can't stand the thought of eating up any organism that might ultimately become a friend. This makes me feel bad, too. I am reduced to a strictly vegetarian diet. I yearn to gobble up a few scrumptiously delicious fat babies, yet I am reduced to struggling through meals of tofu-strips and Loveburger. Oh, if only my conscience would let me feast upon a fat baby just once! But, alas, I am cursed with a very strong conscience."

"Then I am not afraid of you," said Graham. "What about this lion?"

"He is the Cowardly Lion of Oz," explained the Hungry Tiger. "He's got a pretty good conscience, too."

"Then why did he attack me like that?" Graham wanted to know.

"I didn't attack you," replied the Cowardly Lion. "I heard you say that there were some wolves or monsters or something-or-others who were working for the Wicked Witch. You announced that you were going to fight them, so I naturally jumped behind you to cower in fear."

"Oh," said Graham. "I misunderstood your actions."

"So," continued the Lion, "are there really slaves of the W-w-w-witch around here?"

"I heard them talking about how a Witch sent a forest monster and some wolves to attack innocent people," said Graham. "But ..."

"That was us," explained the Tiger. "We like to talk about Oz history a lot. We were in the bushes looking for some yummy kiwi fruits to help satisfy my never-ending hunger when you came along."

"So the Witch isn't after me after all?"

"Guess not," replied the Tiger. "Should she be?"

"Well," he said meekly. "I played a couple of rather crude tricks on her. I suspect that she'll be pretty peeved when she does find me. I left her admiring herself in a … well, a kind of self-induced trance. It's kind of hard to explain. But when she finds a mirror … well, I dread to think what will happen."

The Lion and the Tiger looked at one another. The Lion stood to his full height, which was actually somewhat larger than most of the lions we can see in zoos, and smiled a toothy smile. "I'll protect you, my son!" he snarled. And how he could snarl and smile at the same time was beyond Graham, but let it suffice that he did do it. "No Wicked Witch will get 'hold of any pals of mine! I'm a raging lion, after all! I am big! I am strong! I'm the unchallenged King of the Beasts! I am the—" He dove behind a bush when the Tiger tapped him on the shoulder.

"Er, excuse me," said the Tiger, "but I only wanted to get your attention."

"Sorry," the Lion said meekly, slinking back into the open.

"I think we should learn about our new chum," suggested the Hungry Tiger. "After all, now that you've vowed to protect him, aren't you just a little bit curious as to who he is?"

Graham, seeing that he was expected to introduce himself, told the two cats who he was and how he came to be in Oz, how he had tricked the Witch, and how he met Telly, and how they had conspired together to trick her again, et cetera, et cetera.

The Cowardly Lion shuddered. The Hungry Tiger swallowed hard (an act that normally comes quite easily to him). Even Graham became a little nervous as he recounted his dealings with the Witch and was reminded that he was in imminent danger. "If you two would care to accompany us, you are certainly very welcome," Graham said to the Lion and Tiger.

"Well, I don't know about that," replied the Lion. "At the moment, the old Witch isn't bothering us. And if she sees us with you two, she might decide that birds of a feather flock together, if you know what I mean."

"Oh, don't be such a coward," admonished the Tiger. "She'll see right away that we're not birds."

At that, everyone laughed as the four headed off into the sunset.

CHAPTER TWELVE
THE MEETING WITH PRINCESS OZMA

Graham knew that he would need to have a good plan of action if he was going to get home in spite of the Witch. He looked beseechingly at his two new-found feline friends. Both were certainly both powerful and agile. Still, the boy knew only too well that the four of them were no match for the Wicked Witch. She, after all, had the ability to transport herself to any land she wished. Possibly even to other planets! If she yearned to take them in tow as her prisoners, it seemed impossible to stop her.

"It's terrible!" roared the Cowardly Lion. "I remember when that green Witch appeared at the parade. She scared the living daylights out of me!"

"But," added the Hungry Tiger, "what I can't figure out is why Queen Ozma never did anything about her. She could easily have looked into the Magic Picture to find the villainess, made a wish or two on the Magic Belt, and PRESTO, no more Wicked Witch."

"That's puzzling, indeed," agreed the Cowardly Lion with an obvious shudder. "Could the Witch have done something to Ozma? Maybe Ozma is under some awful spell like she was that time when she lost her memory! Oh, dear oh dear oh dear! We have got to save her!"

"Now let's not jump to any wild conclusions," replied the Tiger, a low growl issuing forth from his stomach. "I suggest that we hurry back to the Emerald City to ask Queen Ozma for her help. If she is under any spells, the Wizard or Glinda will help us. If she is not under any vile enchantment, then her Magic Belt can easily wish away the Witch. She can also send Graham home with the Belt."

"But what if the Witch has enchanted the Wizard and Glinda, too!" bellowed the Lion, tears running down his face. "What if she's made them all into little candy corns or tea bags or Jell-O Jigglers or something?"

The Tiger's stomach roared at the sound of these food words. "Pull yourself together and stop talking about food!" he said. "We can't go losing our heads over things that we don't know for sure. Maybe the whole Witch-thing simply slipped Ozma's mind."

The Cowardly Lion looked at his chum in a reproachful manner. "Tige," he said, "do you really believe that our beloved Queen is so absent-minded? I think we owe her a bit more respect than that. We all saw that repulsive old woman. You saw her, too, Tige! And that th-th-threat! You heard it, t-t-too! No, our Ozma would c-c-certainly have done something to stop that Wicked old W-w-witch by now! And so would Glinda! And the W-w-wizard, too! None of them would have forgotten about all of that! Let alone all th-th-three of th-th-them! No, I can feel it in my bones. She's done something dreadful to them all. They are enchanted or cursed or destroyed or—"

"Are you trying to scare yourself?" said the Tiger.

"I d-d-don't have to try!" wailed the Lion.

"Can't we go to your Emerald City to find out?" asked Graham, who felt that all this talk was doing nothing for anyone. "We have to go there. It's the only way to find out for sure."

"Our young friend has a good head for logic," said the Tiger. "Let's hurry and get to the Emerald City."

The two jungle-cats could move almost as swiftly as the wind. Graham, of course, could not possibly have hoped to keep pace with them had he had to walk on his own. But fortunately, the beasts were willing to allow Graham and Telly to ride upon their backs. This made the journey go much more quickly.

In only a couple of days, the green of the city was in sight. In short order, they got to the front gates which led into this amazing and phenomenally beautiful capital of Oz. Graham could not conceal his awe at the sight of the place.

"Home again," said the Hungry Tiger.

"Now we get to go in and see what poor Ozma and the Wizard have been t-t-turned into!" sighed the Cowardly Lion.

Imby Amby, the Guardian of the Gates, met the trio with a smile of greeting. "Hello!" he said cheerfully.

"Imby," retorted the Tiger, "will you kindly tell my dear boy here that our Queen has not been transformed into a gelatin mold?"

"I should hope not!" replied the Guardian. "Last time I saw her, she was playing checkers with Betsy Bobbin. Seemed to be winning, too."

The Tiger smiled knowingly, then nudged the Lion in a friendly way. "Come on," he said. "Let's go see our Queen. She will certainly set things right straightaway."

The trio hurried into the palace and quickly located the young ruler. She was gaily sipping a cup of herbal tea and having a lively conversation with the Scarecrow and the Patchwork Girl. As soon as she saw her two old friends with the strangers, she stopped in mid-sentence.

"What's wrong?" she asked. "You look upset about something."

The Hungry Tiger bowed low before the little girl. "Your Majesty, this young man, Graham, has come from America and has escaped the clutches of a very wicked Witch. Surely you remember the parade and the horrible threat that this Witch spoke!"

"Surely," replied Ozma. The Patchwork Girl impulsively did five handsprings and landed on the Tiger's broad back, where she proceeded to recite the following in a sing-song voice:

"The Wicked Witch was bad, indeed! Her evil soul was full of greed! To show her powers she did try, and on her broomstick she did fly! She tried to capture everyone; she thought that it would be such fun! But clever Ozma and the Wiz would never let her do this biz! A wholesome spell has now been cast, so that old Witch's time is past. The good old Wizard cast a spell that changed the Witch into a bell! She now can make a bathtub ring, but cannot do another thing!"

Ozma smiled sweetly. "What Scraps is telling you, in her own spirited way, is that your Witch was already dealt with a day or two ago. I saw what she had done in my Magic Picture, and I had the wonderful Wizard of Oz take care of it in his unique manner. He transformed the Witch into a cow-bell. She will remain in that form until such time as she has a change of heart. When she becomes truly repentant and is willing to become a law-abiding citizen of Oz, she will magically become a silver Christmas bell instead of the old cow-bell. At that point, we will restore her to her human form and allow her to live a brand new life as a new and changed individual."

"A cow-bell," echoed the Lion, all trace of fear having suddenly vanished from his heart. "How interesting! I remember a time years ago when the Wizard did a similar trick with some troublesome Imps. He made them into buttons which would change color when they repented."

"Yes," said Ozma. "As for you, friend Telly, I am sure you will become fast friends with the Tin Woodman and Tik-Tok. The two of them are upstairs right now, admiring their similarities and differences. Would you like to have me summon them?"

"Oh, please do!" put in the Scarecrow. "I'd love to see Graham's metal friend meet them. If his heart is as pure as that of my dear friend Nick Chopper's, I know that he will be a very good and wholesome person."

They all agreed and, within minutes, the two metal men stepped into the room. Nick Chopper, the famous Tin Woodman of Oz, had been recently polished, and so was feeling especially bright and chipper. Tik-Tok, who was a clockwork man made out of copper, was always very bright—so long as his clockwork was kept wound up. Telly seemed to be very happy in the company of these new friends.

"I think that it's time to organize a big celebration to commemorate the overthrow of the Wicked Witch and to honor our new friends!" suggested the Patchwork Girl.

"A grand idea!" agreed the Scarecrow.

"And I'd like to hold it in the cabin that Tattypoo made for us near her mountain retreat!" interjected the Patchwork Girl.

"Indeed!" agreed the Scarecrow. "There is plenty of land there. We could have games like potato-sack races and a big parade and a band or two, and...."

"It sounds great!" said Scraps, leaping up, grabbing a chandelier and swinging from it while bursting into song:

> *"A party is the thing to do whenever something pleases you!*
> *I'm awful glad the Witch is belled, for lots of troubles she'd have*
> *spelled! And I am glad to meet young Graham, I hope he won't*
> *think I'm a ham! And Telly is a funny man! I hope he'll be there*
> *if he can! A lovely time we all will spend! We will not want it*
> *e'er to end!"*

She sang in her most dignified manner. Of course, Scraps and dignity are about as compatible as oil and water, but her words were certainly fitting to the occasion.

The celebration was a great success. Celebrities from all over Oz were there. Even the former Good Witch of the North put in an appearance. It was a celebration of nearly the magnitude of that which had caused the arrival of the Wicked Witch in the first place, except that there were no large floats. There had been no time for the Oz folk to construct any. Besides, it seemed to everyone involved that they would not be especially apropos under the circumstances.

When the festivities were over, Ozma approached Graham. "Well," she said in her youthful but queenly voice, "have you enjoyed your little trip to Oz?"

"Oh, yes!" replied the boy. "And I'm so glad to have met you. Wait until I tell my little brother about all of this! He'll be so surprised!"

"Graham," replied Ozma, "you can't tell your little brother about any of the things you've seen here. Even about meeting Dorothy or the Scarecrow."

"But ..." began the boy.

"Graham," she continued, "Oz is a place that would be very interesting to some of the people back in America. So long as they know of Oz as only a fantasy, they will not come to look for us. But our continent and its surrounding regions are very big. Our territory makes your mortal continents look like Rhode Island. Because some mortals do not have your values, and think of no one but themselves or their bank accounts, they would begin to seriously search out our continent. As it comprises so much land, they might eventually break through our magical barriers and invisibility spells—even the spell that diverts them off course whenever they try to reach us. These barriers have been crossed by accident in the past, as you know. If a wicked mortal were trying to do it intentionally, he might find a way."

"But no one has ever done it before," said Graham. "And my brother would so love to hear about Oz. He'd never do anything bad. I promise."

"I am not doubting the righteousness of your brother. But secrets get out, and people pass them along. I know this is true. I cannot allow you to tell anyone back home about Oz being a real place. I want it to be considered only a silly fairy tale for children. This is our greatest protection."

"I understand," said Graham. "I won't tell him about it."

"But you have proven yourself by your love for Telly," said the Queen. "You can stay and live in Oz forever. You will be a citizen here, where you will never have to grow old. You will never again know sickness, and you will never have to die."

Graham was taken aback by the offer. "You mean it?" he said. "I can stay here and be with Telly and the Cowardly Lion and the Hungry Tiger forever?"

"You can."

Graham still seemed overwhelmed. "That would be super," he said. "But... My family! I love my family. Can't you bring them here to live as well?"

"No," Ozma said solemnly. "That is not possible. You are invited only because you have proven your value. Even the Shaggy Man had to prove his worth before staying on in Oz. Your family has not proven itself worthy. You alone may stay in Oz."

"Then I want to go home right now," said Graham. "I can't leave them."

"I thought you'd say that," sighed Ozma. "But you already know too much. I can't send you back there. It isn't that I don't trust you. But I fear that someday you may let the secret slip. Maybe you'd talk in your sleep. Maybe you'd grow older and be taken in by the terrible drugs and alcohol which are so common in the mortal lands. These might make you say things that you'd normally never say. I'm sure it could never happen to a boy like you, but what if… I'm sorry, Graham. You must stay here. I have already arranged for you to have a lovely mansion not far from here. Or you can stay with Telly or whomever you please. You can take any apartments you might desire in the palace if you prefer. In fact, you are free to roam as you please. I don't want to have you think of yourself as a prisoner. I know it will seem that way at first. But I promise you that the benefits of living in Oz will soon drive those ideas from your mind."

Graham looked at Ozma. Any sympathy he might have felt for her was gone. He saw her point, but he did feel more like a prisoner than a citizen of Oz.

CHAPTER THIRTEEN
A WINDOW, A WINDOW

Graham's apartment in the palace was not at all palace-like, and it looked as if it had not been lived in for some time. But he agreed to live there. He had no desire to live in Ozma's palace, but he wanted to have the ability to visit his friends on occasion. He still saw Ozma as a captor. All he had ever wanted was to go home, and now he knew that he was never going to achieve that goal. In his heart, he hated Ozma for doing this to him. The very least she could do would have been to bring his family here! Why was she so structured about things? This was hardly the stuff that nice fairy tales were made of!

Graham's apartment was in a very secluded part of the palace where he would not have to see anyone unless he elected to. There were no neighbors to speak of. Graham sort of preferred it that way. He did not want to speak his mind about the cruel little Queen to anyone. She was so mean that he feared she would make a cow-bell out of him if he seemed the least bit insubordinate.... So he sat in an old settee and brooded. He had a good supply of books to keep him company, and all of the Ozian celebrities had agreed to visit him often. At the time, he had agreed to these visits. But now, as he sat staring at the wall, he wished that they would not come. He yearned only to be left alone. But one can, after all, only be left alone for a short while before he becomes lonesome. And Graham was not so very long in becoming anxious for some sort of companionship, or at least some form of stimulation. He went to a bookshelf and perused the titles on the various tomes that were there. *The Emerald City of Oz* was among them. Graham sullenly took it in his hands and flopped it open. To his astonishment, he found there a reference to Dorothy's aunt and uncle being allowed to come and live in Oz to be close to her. Not only that, but it recounted how Dorothy had come to visit Oz on many occasions, gone back home to Kansas, and even told people about Oz while she was there! This really made Graham feel insulted. If Ozma could trust a girl, why not a boy? For the next couple of hours, Graham pored over the many books that he found in the palace library's vast collection. Each and every time a person, adult, boy, or girl, came to Oz, Ozma had always treated him as she had Dorothy. In fact, the very Shaggy Man that Ozma had mentioned actually had to beg to stay in Oz! Ozma had practically insisted that he be sent home! Why was she acting so cruelly toward himself, but toward no one else? He stood up indignantly and decided then and there to make his way back to the throne room and have a word with Ozma. That mean little girl would have a darn good explanation for this, or she would have a black eye!

Graham walked the corridors of the palace for about twenty minutes. But they seemed to have twisted and turned around. They were not as he remembered them at all. He wondered at this. Could Ozma have done this to permanently entrap him? He grew to hate Ozma more and more as the minutes ticked away. The corridors seemed endless! And none seemed to lead to anyplace in particular, either. "Ooh!" he said, gritting his teeth in frustration. "When I find that little twirp of a Queen, I'm going to show her what-for!" But three more hours of frustration brought him no closer to this goal. At last, he flung himself to the ground and looked up at the ceiling. "I hate you, Princess Ozma!" he grunted. "I hate you!"

Then, from sheer exhaustion, he fell asleep. He remained asleep for an undeterminable period of time. He was awakened by a shaft of light in his eyes. A window! There was a window! He had overlooked it in his frustrated exhaustion, but now it was evident to him. Oh, it was a bit high, but he felt that he might be able to jump up to it. He picked himself up. His body was still a bit exhausted, but he was a young boy. And in good shape. He made his leap. Then he picked himself up and tried again. It took him sixteen tries to make it, but he finally managed to grab hold of the edge of the window. There was no glass, so he pulled himself through. The land outside was a barren mass of crowded prickle-weeds and gnarled old trees. Obviously not a part of the Emerald City that would be mentioned in a travel agent's brochures. But Graham was determined to find Ozma. He pushed aside the prickling weeds as best he could and trudged through the dust and muck of the area. It nauseated him, but he moved on. He thought how odd it was that the Emerald City of Oz would have such an unpleasant area in it. But he let these thoughts dissolve as he recalled what an unpleasant queen the place had. After several hours of fighting against the weeds, most of which were twice his size, he was surprised to hear a small voice. "Who are you?" it said.

"I'm Graham," he replied.

"Really?" said the voice. "I love your crackers. Where are you?"

"I'm in a bunch of weeds," he said.

"Oh? How come?"

"I was trying to find the front of Ozma's palace. Can you help me find it?"

"I could," said the voice. "But you are about four thousand miles out of your way."

"What?" said Graham. "You're wrong! I just escaped out of a window in Ozma's palace a few hours ago! And I know I haven't made any progress hardly at all!"

"I'm afraid it's you who are wrong," replied the voice. "Ozma's palace is a long, long journey from here. Ah, here you are!"

A burst of sudden fire appeared out of nowhere; it burned away a number of the weeds, and Graham saw a clear tunnel through the weeds to open air. In addition to that, however, he saw the most unusual creature he had ever seen … It was not very large, but it looked as if it were composed of several different-sized squares and rectangles. All straight edges, nothing rounded. It had thick, leathery skin, and three glistening hairs grew from the tip of its rectangular tail. The creature spoke: "Now that I have a face to go along with the voice, I can see that you are a stranger in these parts. Allow me to introduce myself. I am he who is called the Woozy. To the best of my knowledge, I am the only Woozy in the world, so I've never had need of any other particular name. Happy to meet you, Graham. I hope that you are a nice fellow, and not some meany who will say Krizzle-Kroo to me."

"N-no," stuttered Graham. "I wouldn't say a thing like that, I'm sure. But—I have just climbed out a window of Ozma's palace. I couldn't possibly be as far from there as you say!"

"Yes, you are," replied the Woozy. "You must be mistaken about the window."

"But Ozma was there! And the Scarecrow, and the Tin Woodman, and the Patchwork Girl, and Tik-Tok, and … and everyone!"

"I'm sorry, my friend Graham," said the Woozy. "There is no palace here. The only building here that I know of is that one that was built by the old Wicked Witch of the West. The Winkies say that she used to have a bunch of winding corridors in there that were meant to drive her slaves nuts if they ever were sent there as a punishment."

"But how did I get there from the Emerald City? Ozma was really mean to me, so I locked myself away in a room there."

"Ozma was mean to you?" the Woozy said with obvious shock. "Are you a villain?"

Graham quickly related the whole story to the Woozy, who seemed to be the only friend (however unfamiliar) he had had around him in an awfully long time.

"My," replied the Woozy. "That is quite a story. But I fear you were duped, my friend."

"Duped?" echoed he.

"I think you were never in the Emerald City. Somehow, the Witch sent you here and created a very elaborate hallucination for you. She uses these weeds for that sometimes. That's why I was burning them away. I can make fire come out of my eyes when I'm angry, and these wicked weeds certainly make me feel that way! Want to see?"

"No," sighed Graham. "So you mean that wasn't Ozma who talked to me?"

"Certainly not!" The Woozy was indignant. "Our dear Queen is not like that at all! I can assure you that you spoke to a hallucination caused by an infusion made out of these dratted weeds!"

"Yes, my little square-boxed squiggley!" came the voice of the Witch. "You have assessed the situation very well." The Witch appeared, seemingly out of nowhere. "Did you really think I was fooled by that ruse? You must think I'm a real moron! But I have won! Telly is disposed of for good!"

"Allidap!" shouted the Woozy. "The fake one from the parade! It's her!" At the sight of the hated individual, a huge blast of fire burst forth from his eyeballs. The Witch ducked aside, but not before getting her face badly blackened and her clothing ruined. "You just wait!" spat the Woozy at the evil creature. "Ozma will look for you in her Magic Picture yet! You just wait! She'll make a spell that will send you away for good!"

"Nope," smiled the Witch. "That's covered. You remember how realistic my illusionary Emerald City was? Well, I watched and waited for a trusted friend of Ozma's to look into that silly old Magic Picture. Then I gave it to him. A very beautiful hallucination! He saw me fall into a river and dissolve completely. So as far as Ozma is concerned, I am destroyed. She'd have no further need to suspect otherwise, so she will not seek me out."

The Woozy was taken aback. But he quickly composed himself and added, "And Glinda will read about you in the Magic Book of Oz!"

"Similarly handled," grinned the Witch. "Any other bright ideas?"

Another blast of fire issued forth from the Woozy's eyes. The weeds went up in a towering inferno.

"Let's get out of here!" said the Woozy to Graham. "Contrary to what some people think, I am not made of wood! I have to breathe, and I fear that this smoke might be as hallucinogenic as the stuff she makes from the weeds!"

The two ran away as fast as they could. At such time as they were far enough from the smoke to breathe easy, Graham stopped running. The Woozy did not seem to notice, and he just kept right on going and going and going. Graham was alone again. But at least he was out of the terrible Witch's reach. Indeed, the Witch was presently having a most exciting dream about plush animals which could be inflated to the size of a house and then used as potato-mashers in the thermostat of life which likes to think about groovy butterflies with red and purple and yellow and violet whispers in the dark backward uprising theme of the way it really was in the thunder of the goat farm with lots of yams and a shovelful of fine white powder that looked like the side of a barn with lots of clocks and fleas with orange earrings in their hazy green and blue and pink walking-sticks which were married to some tortilla chips and about thirty-five orange and brown cabinet-makers with green feathers and pink fur.

CHAPTER FOURTEEN
JEANNE-MARIE

Graham sat down upon the ground and sighed. He was glad to have escaped from the Wicked Witch yet again, but he felt sorry for his companion. He wondered what that awful old woman might have done to poor Telly. Could she have locked him away in a torture chamber someplace? Some terrible winding maze such as he had just left? It made him feel sick to even imagine it. He absently sat and drew a picture of Telly in the dirt. "Where are you, Telly?" he asked aloud. He spoke his question into the air, and no answer seemed to be forthcoming. "What has she done to you? I have to know. I miss you, Telly! You are my best friend in this strange land. I love you! Where have you been taken?"

"Who is Telly?" came an unfamiliar female voice. Graham turned about to see who had spoken. He was looking as much into the sun as into the face of the speaker. It was hard to distinguish her features. But she looked like a fine white horse.

"Hello?" said Graham uncertainly.

"Hello," replied the voice. Whoever she was, she sounded gentle and understanding. "My name is Jeanne-Marie. Why are you so glum?"

"My friend has been taken prisoner by a bad Witch," explained the boy, who felt an inexplicable trust for this equine newcomer. "Oh," she replied. "I am sorry. I had thought that Queen Ozma had done away with all such vile Witches."

"Well," he sighed, "she doesn't know about this one. This wicked old Witch has created a very clever illusion that has made Ozma unable to see her or to find out about her. I was fooled, too. I had been under the impression that Ozma was as wicked as the Witch. But I was wrong. If only I could find Ozma. The real Ozma, not just an illusion that was passing itself off as the real Ozma. Then I could tell her what was going on. If all that the Woozy told me is true, the real Ozma would be able to make things right again. As it is, I can't help Telly, and I can never go home to America again, either!"

The horse nestled down beside the boy. Only then did he realize that this was no normal horse that was speaking to him. She was different from all horses in all Graham's experience. She was as pure white as the driven snow, and her mane was a shiny silver. From the top of her head grew a long, beautiful horn. "Wow!" exclaimed Graham. "Are you a real unicorn?"

"So I've been told," laughed Jeanne-Marie. "But I am a long way from my home, just like you are. I left that area because the other unicorns didn't seem to understand my views on things. They thought I was strange and that I was not worthy of the name of the unicorns. But I cannot help what I am. I yearn to see all that there is to see of this Land of Oz in which I live. And I wanted to find someone who could understand my philosophies, too. None of the stallions of my breed took me seriously, and I have never once felt true love. At least, not until I met MacDonald Lindsay."

"Who is that?" wondered Graham.

"Well, I haven't actually met him in person," she admitted. "But I overheard him talking to his helpers one day. He was telling them about the need for all sentient beings to have a purpose in life. No one can be fulfilled if he is not in some way making his existence count for anything. He himself is in control of the finest dairy farm in Oz. He has vast fields of milkweed that his helpers harvest for him in exchange for their housing, food, and the occasional game of quoits."

"That sounds fair, I suppose," replied Graham, realizing that this group was not one which was accustomed to using any form of money.

"Very much so," she said. "And the helpers—a unique tribe of warthog-like amphibians known as wartfrogs—are highly contented with their lot. MacDonald Lindsay allows them to come and go as they please, and he has given each of them a home that is far more luxurious than his own little lodging. Actually, MacDonald's farm is the only thing he has that is luxurious. His personal abode is a simple cleft in a rock that you can see from here in that little hill." She pointed with her horn.

"I see it," said Graham. "This MacDonald fellow sounds like a good enough guy."

"Oh, he is very good," said Jeanne-Marie. "But very mysterious. I have not had any real opportunity to ask him, but I think I could be very happy working in his fields alongside the wartfrogs."

"Have you ever tried to go to him to ask for a job?" questioned Graham.

"No. But I have been in his fields. Indeed, his milkweed is the best in all the land. It is not just an ordinary dairy-farm product. It is special. It is chocolate milkweed, and it is as smooth as Chinese silk. I have been following the wartfrogs and sneaking an occasional taste of any chocolate milkweed pods that they overlooked."

"I see," said Graham.

"You are welcome to have dinner with me," said Jeanne-Marie. "I have at least a half-dozen pods that I am willing to share with you."

It was at that point that Graham remembered how long it had been since last he had eaten. Even then, he was not sure the food had been anything more than an illusion conjured up by the Witch. It was not more than a second before he heard himself accepting the invitation. Indeed, the chocolate milkweed was the most delicious thing Graham had ever tasted. He thanked Jeanne-Marie over and over for sharing this delightful new taste-treat with him. He and the unicorn talked for a long while afterward. He was not sure just how long it was, but he awoke the next morning feeling quite refreshed.

The unicorn had already gone on her way. But she had left a note for Graham explaining that she had gone to watch the wartfrogs in MacDonald Lindsay's fields, as was her usual morning activity. The note informed him that she would seek him out later that afternoon, if he cared to stay in the vicinity, and that she was happy to have met him should he choose to move on…

After thinking it over, Graham decided that he was going to need help if he planned to rescue poor Telly from the false Allidap. Hence, he decided to wait for Jeanne-Marie. He could spend the day formulating a plan that would allow them to get Telly away from the Witch without endangering their own lives.

MacDonald Lindsay was a fellow who was in high position on his farm, yet he gave all of the finest of his yield to others. He was a man who had few needs, only the knowledge that his crops were bringing happiness to others. That was all he had ever asked. Yet there was something missing in his life. Something upon which he could not place a finger. Yes, indeed MacDonald Lindsay had fingers. Three of them on each hand, in fact! He was a powerful and muscular troll, for all intents and purposes. That is, he was from the waist up. From his waist down, instead of the usual troll waist and legs, however, he had the neck and body of a mighty black stallion. Anyone born under the astrological sign of Sagittarius might recognize him as a relation to the centaur. But MacDonald Lindsay claimed no such heritage formally. "Lambert," he said, putting a beefy hand on the shoulder of one of his workers, who happened to be a foreman among the wartfrogs.

"Yeah?" asked the amphibian.

"Who is the little unicorn? The one I see out there in my fields? I have seen her other times, too."

"I know no name for her," sighed the wartfrog. "My boys and I have seen her before, though. She only takes a few pods—and only those extreme few that my boys don't consider worthy of picking or trading in your name. Those that she takes are all too small or have already been picked over by the crows. We had once considered making a scarecrow—an inanimate one, of course. Not like the guy who usually comes to mind when we think of scarecrows. But that little unicorn seems to get what she needs from our leftovers, so no one has bothered to send her on her way."

"So she only takes that which is rejected from my farm?" replied MacDonald doubtfully.

"Well," began the worker, "please don't be angry with me. There have been a couple of occasions that I have taken pity on the poor creature and left a few better pods for her to find. Please don't get angry, sir! I only did it because I felt sorry for the poor little thing. She looked so hungry, and we have so much."

Within minutes, the mighty centaur-like man was looking into the eyes of the young unicorn. "I—I'm sorry to intrude on your farm," she said tremblingly.

"Listen, my dear," he said. "You are welcome in my fields any time you wish to be here. You are welcome to take any milkweed you want or to help yourself to any of my other crops. I have asked my wartfrogs to ignore you. You no longer need to feel like an intruder."

"You are very kind," she replied. "You know that I am not from around here. I am not understood amongst my own kind, so I am something of an outcast, you might say."

"Not here, you're not."

"Thank you, sir!" The unicorn seemed to be near tears. "Thank you so much!"

When Jeanne-Marie returned to the little clearing where she had left Graham, she brought him several milkweed pods, as well as a few cookies she had picked from the bushes around the base of MacDonald's rock. "He is very sweet," she said. "The moment I saw his eyes, I knew that he was special. Graham, do you believe in love at first sight?"

"I don't know," he said to her. "But I sure do love these cookies!"

And so it went for the next day and the next. By day, Jeanne-Marie went to the fields, where she grew more and more fond of the odd stallion there. By night, she plotted with Graham as to how they might go about locating Telly. The problem seemed to be that the Witch could have magically zapped him off as far away as Santa Monica, California, had she wanted to do so. Finding him would not be an easy task. To make matters worse, poor Jeanne-Marie had become a tad too taken with MacDonald Lindsay. The wartfrogs had begun to mistrust her.

"She isn't even the same kind of animal!" said Lambert, the wartfrog leader. "She doesn't have any troll features—not even a little around the eyes! They are totally incompatible! She must only be out to get his milkweed! To think that I once felt sympathy for that wretched little unicorn! Why, that cunning little crook even has Lindsay entranced so much that he has begun giving her some of the good stuff! She is no longer contented with the scraps and rejects of our fields! She has got to go. But how shall we do it? It will have to be handled in a sneaky enough way so as to keep Lindsay from noticing. He has been placed under the spell of that little siren, and I know that he would never grant us permission to shove her away from the area."

It was the very next day that the wartfrogs made their move. Under the direction of Lambert, they went about their work, and it was business as usual. Then, when one of the amphibious pigs saw the small unicorn in the field behind them, Lambert called for a halt. The wartfrogs turned around and went back toward Jeanne-Marie. She was not looking in their direction, so she did not notice that they were coming toward her until it was too late to escape. They were already upon her and hurled her unceremoniously into a harvesting-bag. This they tossed onto their cart and carried away. "I will sell her to a zoo in some other land, where they are not so kind to thieving horse-creatures!" giggled Lambert, showing his teeth. "Now we can get rid of this little troublemaker once and for all! Old Mickey-D will never know what became of his dear little charity-case!"

Indeed, it would have been curtains for poor Jeanne-Marie had not Graham had a sudden inspiration which he wanted to tell her about right away. He felt certain that he had formulated a plan by which they would be able to save Telly from the Witch, and he had run into the milkweed fields to find her. He had seen the terrible wartfrogs capture her and had even overheard what they planned to do to her. "I can't let them do it!" he whispered angrily. "Why, this is the second time I've made a friend in Oz who has met with foul play!" He would have cried, had his sadness not been so highly overcompensated for by his anger. His first instinct was to run to her and try to fight for her freedom. But he was a wise enough boy to know full well that this would be folly. He was no more than one little boy against a whole farm's worth of strong and muscular laborers. If he were to pick a fight with this bunch, he would be sold alongside his friend. No, he would need another plan of rescue. But he had already come up with one such plan. Now he could give it a test-run. However, he knew that he could not hope to carry it out all by himself. No, he would have to have help. And Graham knew from whence that help must come. With a swallow of anxiety, he headed for the home of the ranchero.

MacDonald Lindsay was as amiable a fellow as the unicorn had said. This fact instantly put Graham's anxiety to rest. "Do come in, my friend," said the ranchero. "What can I do to make you happy?"

"It's about Jeanne-Marie," said Graham.

"That poor little waif of a unicorn?" replied the troll-horse.

"That very one," said Graham. "Your workers have taken her prisoner, and they plan to sell her to a zoo or a circus or something like that."

The troll creature looked at Graham and frowned. Then he began to laugh. "Ha ha!" he said. "You take me for a complete and utter idiot! No, you cannot be telling me the truth. My boys are under orders to let the lovely little waif alone. They would not do such a cruel or vile thing to anyone, I assure you."

"But I was there, sir," pleaded Graham. "I saw it all with my own two eyes! They put Jeanne-Marie into a great big grain-bag and hid her on a cart that they carried along behind them. The big fat one said he was going to sell her to a zoo! I heard him say so! He said, 'Old Mickey-D will never know what became of his little charity-case!'" As he quoted the line, he did his best to imitate the wartfrog's voice. "Please, Mr. Lindsay, you just have to believe me! I'm telling you the truth!"

"Now, now," answered the troll voice, which was sounding less patient than before. "I know better. No one on my staff would ever do such a thing … And no one on my staff would ever … Wait a minute. Did you say 'Old Mickey-D?' My, my. Only Foreman Lambert ever called me by that annoying name. And no one but he would have the audacity to...." His heart pounded so loudly that Graham could hear it from across the room. Then the troll-horse let out a couple of loud exclamations. "Merciful Frances of Grand Rapids, Minnesota!" he bellowed. "Judy in the sky! What a fool I have been to overlook it! Lambert has been trying to hide it from me, but he has been showing signs of resentment against that unicorn! I should have seen this coming. But you have opened my eyes, my boy. I have strived—er, striven? Er, I have always made it my strivence in these fields to ensure that every visiting child and family successfully explores his own particular creative abilities. I had seen so many fine qualities of leadership in Foreman Lambert that I closed my eyes to his darker side. But I can no longer look the other way. It may not be kosher, but I am going to have to fight against my own right-hand man."

The ranchero started angrily for the door.

"Wait!" shouted Graham, taking on the role of the calm and collected boy with a plan.

"Wait for what?" asked Lindsay. "I'll wait for nothing until I see that lousy Lambert get his just rewards!"

"He will," spoke the boy. "Yes. But not that way!"

"What ..."

"If you try to fight all of those thugs at once, you'll just be outnumbered. I have a better idea. I know of a way to save Jeanne-Marie without anyone getting hurt."

"Then spill it, my boy! What is this plan?"

Foreman Lambert took the rest of the day off. He carefully researched the best place to sell a captured unicorn. He planned to get enough wealth to buy the entire farm and spend the rest of his days sipping strawberry daiquiris and conversing with MacDonald Lindsay about the joys of being affluent. As he sat and pored over the pages of *The Encyclopedia of Places Where Unicorns Can be Successfully Sold on the Black Market With No Questions Asked Except When the Salesman Happens to be a Mangaboo: Vol. 224*, he heard a peculiar clattering noise outside. Fearing it might affect his own happiness in some way, Lambert ran outside to see what was the matter. The sight that met his eyes was hardly what he would have expected. There before him was a huge Ox tethered to a wagon. One wheel had fallen from the wagon, and the wagonmaster was jumping up and down, shouting angry expletives at the ox. "You filthy pile of oxtail soup!" shouted the young man. "You are as able to locate the proper roads as Dorothy was in *The Road to Oz*! Now just look what your lack of brains has caused us! You dragged us off the road, and now we have another busted wheel to bother about! You are just a lousy old coot!"

"Now, now," said Lambert. "You needn't speak so unkindly to this fine animal. I'll be happy to take him off your hands if he's such a … a coot, I think you said?"

"Yeah!" begged the ox. "Let him have me! I can work on this big farm!"

"Not a cotton-picking chance!" blurted the human. "I need a work-horse to pull this wagon. If I had another animal, maybe a horse or a pony, I'd gladly unload your crummy old worthless hide in a heartbeat! But such beasts are sure to be expensive in these parts, especially to a stranger like me. And all I have are these forty-eight diamonds, a bag of square emeralds, and a couple of rubies to spare."

Lambert lit up and became more alert than he had ever been before. Standing straight up and trying to look as businesslike as a wartfrog can possibly look, he said, "That is the exact price I planned to ask for a very pretty unicorn that I have recently acquired by perfectly legitimate means."

"Are there any other kind?" asked the stranger with a sly wink.

"Of course not." He ran inside to the closet and grabbed the bag with Jeanne-Marie inside. Coming back to his customer, he handed it over and greedily grabbed the precious gemstones. "Thank you, oh thank you!" he squealed gleefully. "And can I get that ox, too?"

"You can get me, all right," said the ox. "But I'm not sure you want what comes with me." Stepping toward the wartfrog and ramming his face against one of Lambert's tough tusks (which, consequently, broke off and fell to the ground), he broke off what became obviously a papier maché mask. Beneath it, he was actually the owner of the whole ranch, MacDonald Lindsay.

"Oh oh…." gasped Lambert. "Er, hi, master. I knew it was you all along. That is why I went along with your silly little game. Had it been anyone but you, I'd not have left my work for a moment to play such a game. But no harm done, right? Here, take these little gemstones away. I don't really need them. All part of the game, though, you know. Well, I do have work to do now … Toodle-oo!"

"LAMBERT!" roared the troll in a voice that would have shamed the kingliest of lions. "You have no work to do here."

"Oh, but I do," said Lambert. "I must take this darling unicorn back to where she belongs. Oh, yes, yes! Please do not hinder us. I must get her away from here, where she is such a lovely distraction. Yeah, that's exactly the problem, my master. Gotta get her home now. Later!"

The troll placed a powerful and majestic hoof on one of Lambert's flippers. "Excuse me," he said. "But I told you that you have no further work to do here. Please pick up your toys and get off of my ranch. And take your disobedient helpers with you. Also, you may have as many milkweed pods as you can carry. I'll never let it be said that I am heartless."

"But, master!" stammered Lambert. "You can't do this! You mustn't! We've come such a long way already! I was up for a raise next year!"

"I'll raise a few things for you if you aren't out of my sight before nightfall." Lindsay was suddenly calm. "And if I ever see you around this innocent waif again, I will … Well, I don't rightly know what I'll do. But you can rest assured that it won't be very much fun for either of us."

CHAPTER FIFTEEN
CAN'T STAND IN THE WAY OF LOVE

"Well, now!" cackled the Witch. "You thought you'd seen the last of ol' Allidap, did you? You were so wrong! Ha ha ha! Now I have you in my clutches once more, and you won't be escaping from me again, I can tell you! To think, you tried to trick me with a photo of some television star. But you won't be able to fool me again quite so easily, my little basket of nuts and bolts!"

The evil woman had chained Telly to a large black platform and was standing over him in a most menacing manner. "You showed me a picture of somebody else to make me think I was a ravishing beauty. You lied to me, you electronic hunk of junk!"

Telly struggled to free himself of his chains, but they proved to be too strong for him. Giving in, he stopped struggling and tuned in to an old rerun of *Walt Disney's Wonderful World of Color*.

"Let me see now," muttered the false Allidap. "I must think this over. I have to do something appropriate to punish you for your deceptive ways. Maybe I should turn you into a candy cane and gobble you up?" She scratched her chin. "No, that would be much too kind. I must think of a punishment that is more fitting to a ROTTEN, MEAN LIAR such as you happen to be. Hmmm. Maybe I could transform you into a little brown wart on the left foot of a slimy old toad? Or a bucket of rotten peas? But that still seems hardly enough punishment for a creepy little crawler like you. Oooh! Of all the disgusting luck! If I had only been manifested with the ability to read! Then I could find a perfectly lovely little spell to cast on you that would satisfy my need to punish you!" She stalked to a nearby shelf which was covered with various bottles of herbs and tinctures. Each of these had a faded yellowing label, but none of these labels did her any good. It became clear to her that the inability to read was indeed a great setback. As she pondered an appropriate course of action, she heard a rustling sound outside. "What is that annoying noise?" she spat. "Maybe your little pal Graham has come to let me capture him as well? I will make short work of him, let me tell you! He was a fool to come here!" She stepped lively to the door and stamped her way outside. "Okay, little boy!" she called. "I know that you are out here someplace! Come on out of hiding. Trying to trick me will only make it worse on yourself. Come to me quietly, and let us get this messy ordeal over with quickly. Being that you are so fond of reading Oz books, I think I will turn you into a copy of *Dorothy and the Wizard in Oz*. Then, as a book does me no good, I will toss you into my fireplace and watch you burn!"

There was no reply.

"I see," sighed the Witch. "So you want to make things difficult, do you? Well, I am willing to go along with your silly little game of hide-and-go-seek. But just remember, my fine and dandy little gentleman, that once I do find you, I will not be so lenient on your crummy hiding little hide!" As she searched the scraggly brush that surrounded her home, she grew more and more agitated. "You may be a pretty good hider," she bellowed. "But I'll get you in the end, you just wait and see!" She searched for a solid half hour before she decided that Graham was not to be found. "The little fruitcake must have run off in fear and horror," she determined. "Well, I will concern myself with his punishment some other time. Right now, I have the television set to attend to. I will miss my soaps, but I think it's high time I put that nasty old creep in his proper place. I think I'll make him into a nice bowl of lumpy spider-flavored oatmeal and have him for a snack." So saying, she sauntered back into her home. Once inside, she was met with a sight that made her more angry than ever. There, on either side of the platform which held Telly captive, were the two huge jungle-cats. The Cowardly Lion was trying in vain to unshackle Telly's chains. The Hungry Tiger, who had been standing guard, saw the enemy and instantly prepared to spring on her. "You'd better leave us alone, you yucky old Witch!" growled the Tiger threateningly. "We are taking Telly to the real Emerald City to meet the real Queen Ozma. Once Ozma hears what you've been up to, she'll transport you to some place where you can never cause our beloved Land of Oz any further grief!"

"Is that so?" chuckled the Witch, quickly regaining her bearings. "I'd like to see the stumbling, demented child queen try that! Maybe I should turn her into a toadstool to show you that I am the all-powerful one here. Your foolish little girl is no queen! She's just a flimsy excuse for a bad one-liner. In fact, you know what I'm going to do to her? I think I should enjoy making her into a little sugar cube and drinking her in my tea. But first, I think I should take care of you little kitty cats. I have heard a story about a little brat named Sambo who made some tigers into butter. I think this tawny scrawny beast would be a fine spread for my toast. Yes, I think that should be quite delicious. And the little lion could become the toast! How delightful it would be to eat the two of you together!"

The Lion was visibly shaken by this idea. "I d-d-don't want to be t-t-toast!" he bellowed fearfully.

"And I will not become a pat of butter, either," added the Tiger, quickly springing on the antagonist and knocking her over.

The Witch struggled for a few minutes and finally freed herself, only to be knocked over a second time by the Lion, who had summoned up a few grams of courage in just the nick of time. "You pestery creatures!" she blurted. "You filthy rotten haggard beasts of bumbling stumbling stupidity! I will see you both destroyed and I'll laugh about it, you rotten dirty crummy hateful old things!" Summoning in her rage a strength she had never before known, she hurled the Lion on top of the Tiger. Then, grabbing a huge net, she threw it over the two of them before they had any time to move out of the way. "Now I have you all, my dearies! All three of that foolish kid's friendies! And I'll see you all into your demises right now!" the Witch said in a whisper. She was about to carry out this threat when there was a knock on the door. "Oh, drat it all!" said the Witch. "Who could that be? If it's your silly Scram-Graham, I'll allow him the honor of watching me destroy all of the rest of you!" She went to the door. There, she saw a strange creature looking at her and wearing a painted smile on his face. "What the dickens are you?" she said. "You look a little bit like a troll, but you have a horse's body growing out of your waist."

"I am a sort of horse-troll," he replied. "But that is not important right now. What is important is that this may be your lucky day!"

"My lucky what?" asked the Witch, not quite understanding.

"Is this the home of Bastinda Slinky Myrna Evillene Allidap?" asked the stranger.

"Er ... I guess so," replied the Witch.

"Splendid!" replied the ranchero. "And would you happen to be Bastinda Slinky Myrna Evillene Allidap?"

"I think so," she said, not sure she remembered all of those names that were being applied to her.

"Delightful!" said the stranger. "Then I am here, Ms. Allidap, to tell you that today is the luckiest day of your life!"

"Is it?"

"Indeed so! Ms. Allidap, you were selected out of the five hundred billion applicants to receive a prize of twenty-seven million dollars and thirteen cents! And, since you were home when I arrived, you may be eligible for more prizes!" He turned around and whistled through his teeth. "Oh, boys! She's here. Bring in the cameras." A small, horse-like creature and a young man with a television camera in place of a head came running up. "Oh, good. You're here. Mr. Camerahead, let's get some good footage of our lucky winner in her home. Let's go inside. It will look more natural if our winner is in a comfortable place on her sofa."

"But …" began the Witch. "But … I didn't even know there was a TV station in Oz."

"Well, of course there is," said the horse. "Where else would Ozites turn to see their favorite Rankin-Bass Oz cartoon episodes? We are broadcasting from the peak of Some Summit. Now, come on, let's be lively about this. We haven't got all day. We have a commercial to shoot for *The Ozmapolitan* newspaper at ten after three."

"Why don't you stand here in front of your television set?" suggested the camera man. "But we'll have to unchain it from this thing here. This won't look pleasing to our television audience."

"No!" raged the fake Allidap. "Leave that alone!"

But the camera man, who had come equipped with some heavy-duty metal clippers, had Telly freed in no time at all. "Now, my dear Ms. Allidap," said the centaur. "Please stand still and try to look surprised. If this all goes well, you may be eligible for an all expense paid trip to Walt Disney World in Tampa, Florida. That's in the United States, you know. So it may be possible for you to meet the President and give him any advice you might have for him."

"But…. Hey…." stuttered the Witch.

"You want him to butt some hay?" said the horse. "I think I'd rather eat it than butt it. But to each his own. I think we need some extra color in this place. It looks too gloomy." She picked up a bucket (which had been carried in by the centaur) in her teeth and began to splash some rainbow-colored paint all about the room, some of which went directly into the Witch's eyes. Allidap tried to cry out in rage, but she only got some paint in her mouth.

"This looks great!" said the camera man. "The color really adds a lot. The people watching will be happier to see it than the gloominess that used to be here. Now, let me see… Let's have some creative banter. Ms. Allidap, can you look excited and happy? Come on, let's see that beautiful smile."

"Yes," added the centaur. "And hop up and down screaming, 'I won! I won!' if you think you can handle it."

The Witch was having trouble following all of this—especially with the paint in her eyes that made it impossible to see anything around her. But she did like the thought of having won something, so she did her best to do as they asked. When they seemed satisfied with their TV footage, they bid her a fond adieu and scurried out the door.

Once a good distance from the Witch's home, the camera man took off his mask. Of course, as you may have already guessed, it was actually Graham in disguise. And with him were MacDonald Lindsay and Jeanne-Marie. The plan had worked, and they had rescued not only Telly, but also the Cowardly Lion and the Hungry Tiger as well.

"I want to thank you," said Telly, "for coming to our rescue that way. That was a clever trick, making the Witch think you were there to put her on television. I wouldn't have actually wanted to televise an image of her, as it might damage my picture tube, but it worked."

The Cowardly Lion and the Hungry Tiger thanked them as well.

"I think we should be looking for the real Ozma," said Graham. "The Witch will eventually be out hunting me down again."

"A good thought," agreed the Hungry Tiger. "We shall go and find her straightaway."

The centaur looked solemn. "I would so love to meet our dear ruler," he said. "But I fear I may be in for a rude visit from those wartfrogs, and I think I should be there when it comes to pass. However, I will join you in the Emerald City as soon as I have sent the wartfrogs away for good. I will be sorry to be apart from this dear unicorn, however. We have been talking, and we agree that we belong together. I will be anxiously looking forward to seeing her again very soon."

"No," replied Jeanne-Marie. "I shall come back to the farm and help you to rid yourself of those former employees of yours. Then we shall travel together to the Emerald City."

This was a sad parting for all, after all of the adventures they had shared together. But it was as it had to be. So they all said their good-byes and parted, and the two equine-type creatures headed in one direction and the four mismatched friends in the other.

CHAPTER SIXTEEN
A STORY WITH A HAPPY ENDING

The four friends had reached a clearing behind which a clump of trees partially camouflaged a quaint little cottage. By this time Graham was feeling quite thirsty and thought it would be a good idea to knock on the cottage door and see if he could obtain a nice drink of water. The cottage was surrounded by a garden full of flowers and a white picket fence, and it was all so pretty it could have come right out of a fairy tale. Graham knew full well that no evil person could possibly reside in such a picturesque place, so he boldly opened the gate and walked along the little winding path to the front door, where he knocked loudly.

A minute went by with no response, whereupon Graham knocked again, but this time quite a bit louder.

"Why don't you just knock my door down?" said a voice behind him. Graham about jumped out of his skin as he spun around to see a very kindly lady with a twinkle in her eyes approaching from the back of the house. "I was pruning my roses in the back garden," she continued, "when I heard what I thought must be a very rude person banging on my front door. I gather you must be here on a very urgent matter."

"Well … not exactly," Graham said rather sheepishly. "I was feeling very thirsty and thought that perhaps I might be able to obtain a drink of water"

"Hmmm, I think that can be arranged," replied the lady. "And what about your friends?" she asked, looking rather curiously at Telly and a little nervously at the Lion and Tiger.

"Oh, Telly here is an electrical-mechanical person and is not very partial to water. But if you could wipe his face with a damp cloth, he'll not only look better and be able to see better, but I'll be able to see his television programs better. Would you like to watch one now?"

The lady was more than a little confused by this invitation, but she obliged by spraying some glass cleaning liquid on Telly's screen and wiping it with a dry cloth. "Ouch! That stuff stings my eyes!" Telly protested loudly. But he was happy that all of the dust had been removed from his screen.

"How about the lion and tiger?" asked the lady. "Would they like a drink? They don't bite, do they?" Without waiting for an answer, the lady led them to the back of the house, where a well was located. She hauled up a bucket of ice-cold, crystal clear water, which Graham took a long drink of from a ladle which she handed to him. The Lion and Tiger said they were not thirsty, but the Tiger asked politely if there were any fat babies residing with her. Graham coughed and choked as the water went down the wrong way. Fortunately, the noise drowned out the Tiger's question, and the lady did not hear him …

With his thirst more than satisfied, Graham proceeded to introduce himself and did his best to explain his current situation and Telly's unique abilities. The lady replied that her name was Doré and that she was both an artist and a storyteller. She then went into the house and brought out several unique pen and ink drawings, as well as some beautiful watercolors, which everyone greatly admired. She looked intently at the Hungry Tiger and said he was a magnificent animal and that she would like to sketch him. The Tiger could not resist smirking at the Lion, who just rolled his eyes.

"Now," continued Doré as she sketched away, "I'll tell you one of my stories if you like."

Graham and his friends nodded vigorously. After all, they all loved to hear stories. Everyone sat down on the soft velvety grass by the well as Doré proceeded to tell the story. She had no sooner started when lots of little animals appeared as if from nowhere and gathered around to listen. They somehow knew that there was nothing to fear from the Lion or the Tiger.

"The title of my story," said Doré, "is 'Helen's Smile.' I hope you like it:

Today was a special day. Not only because the sun was shining, but because he felt good. It had been a long time since he had felt so good. He sat in his chair on the porch as he had done every single day throughout winter, summer, fall, and (his favorite time of the year) spring.

He was a people-watcher all right. No question about that. And almost everyone in town had to pass his house on the way to the train station. He liked that. He knew who worked in the city, who was late, and who went in early. You could tell a lot about people by the schedules they kept. This was a particularly beautiful day. Fall nipped the air, and it felt crisp to the skin. The leaves were just hinting at the change in colors. He liked this time of the year almost as much as he liked spring. The heat of the summer had a way of sapping a man's strength. Fall was different; there was something about the cool air that made his blood surge through his body. Food seemed to taste better, and the air smelted especially clean. The women seemed to look prettier than ever. Yes, sir! This was a good time of the year. His name was Clive, and he was only twenty-seven years old. He had never really lived in the usual sense of the word, but he was wise beyond his years. People always waved and said "Hi" to him, but few approached him. They knew he was a handicapped person because he was always in his wheelchair, and you would think people would want to chat and be cheerful around him so he would feel good, but few ever did. It was his face that bothered them. It was deformed. This was a source of great pain to his mother, who always carried a cloak of guilt about her. His eyes were set very far apart and bulged. Many of the children on their way to school called him "Frog." They'd shout, "Hey, Froggy-Froggy! Hey, Mr. Frog!" and make loud croaking sounds. They never knew the pain it caused him. A few children, however, were far more sensitive and loving and would wave and smile and sometimes come right up to him and say, "Hi, Clive. How are you today?" This made him feel happy again.

Clive's mouth was large and hung loosely at the ends. Somehow nature had forgotten to give him all his facial muscles. For all his many emotions, his face only reflected one. To watch him try to smile was painful. His shriveled body was even sadder to observe. This day, Clive sat and watched Helen pass by. He thought she had to be the most beautiful person in the world. Surely a prettier girl could not exist. He watched her intently, as he had done for the past six years. She walked by and did not look his way, as usual. She always knew he was there. She had sneaked a peak at him once and was so repulsed that she could not bring herself to look again. Yet she knew how he felt about her. She could feel it as she walked by. At first she felt afraid passing by. She even tried taking a different route to the station. But after a while she felt silly. So she passed his house with her head held high and her eyes straight ahead.

As the years passed, she found out about the "cripple" who sat on his porch all day. It was a sad story: Apparently, the father couldn't cope with a deformed baby, so he deserted the family. The mother was a simple country-girl. She was forced to take in wash and to clean other people's houses. But she managed to support herself and her deformed child. She was a quiet woman who minded her own business. She rarely spoke. But she could polish silver and furniture like no other person and so she had plenty of work. In time, she was able to afford her own house. They had lived in that house on Mulberry Street for twenty years. It was always clean and neat. On rare occasions, Helen saw the mother shopping. The mother was so thin and gaunt. How did she manage to lift that son of hers?

As Helen passed the house that bright fall morning, she wondered if the man could stand up or walk. "Helen! Helen! You look so pretty today!" The young woman stopped dead in her tracks. Who spoke? She looked around her. No one that she could see was there—except the person on the porch. Was it him? No … It couldn't be. She had heard that he knew how to speak, but that he was very difficult to understand. But this voice was pleasant and articulate. Very masculine, too. *Is someone hiding behind a bush? No. I'm being silly*, she thought. *I must have imagined it.* She looked around one more time, yet carefully avoiding looking at the figure on the porch.

"Helen, why do you always ignore me?"

Again she stopped. This time she did not look around. She knew. "Yes. You are right. It is me. I have finally gotten up enough courage to talk to you. It has taken me years. Can't you turn around just this once and smile at me? It won't hurt you. You are so lovely, more lovely than even the moon, the stars, and all the flowers in the world. Today I am going to die. Yes! Really! I am so happy. It is such a special day. I knew I was going to die three days ago, and I prayed to God that, before I died, I could just see Helen smile. He gave me the 'gift' of speaking into your mind for just this one special day. And He promised that I could speak articulately if what I said came from the heart. I know you can hear me. Please. I love you so much … Won't you turn and smile at me? Just this once?"

Helen stood rooted to the spot. She knew she was experiencing something abnormal. She was frightened. *How does he know he is going to die? That's impossible! But it's also impossible to hear a voice inside your head, and I know I'm hearing it! Oh, God! Dare I do it? Can I look at him? He's so ugly—so unbearably ugly! But how sad. It was a beautiful thing he said to me. What if I do smile? Will he expect me to smile every day? No! I can't do that. Next he'll ask me to come up to the porch and chat. I couldn't bear it. I couldn't!* Yet her heart went out to him. *What loneliness he must feel. I'll smile just this once, and then tomorrow I'll take the other route.* She gathered all her willpower and slowly turned around, smiling. At that moment she could feel a tremendous surge of love radiate towards her and envelope her entire being. The sun was shining so brightly that it momentarily blinded her, so she really couldn't see his face, but nevertheless she kept smiling for a moment or two. Then she turned and continued on her way.

It was now several weeks since she had changed her route. By now she was convinced that she had only imagined the voice. Yet she could not bring herself to walk down his street again. It was another glorious day. Helen had the day off and was going shopping. She was standing at the checkout counter when she felt a light touch on her arm. She turned and drew in her breath. It was HIS mother!

"Hello," said the mother in a soft voice. "I don't want to trouble you, but I just want to tell you something I promised my son before he died."

Helen's heart skipped a beat. "He died?"

"Yes, dear. He died several weeks ago. He had been sitting out on the porch as usual when he called out to me and told me you had smiled at him. Dear, you made him so happy. He asked me to tell you something. Then he slumped over and died. Just like that. Don't feel sad, dear. It was a blessing. He did not believe that death was the end. He believed that he would receive a fine new body."

"What did he say?"

The mother looked up at her, the most pleasant smile crossing her face. "He said to thank you for your smile. And to tell you that someday he will meet you again and it will be a different story. Your smile made his life worthwhile, and he died a very, very happy man."

Helen felt a sadness creeping over her. *It was only a smile,* she thought. *Now I am sorry I didn't smile before. It was such a little thing for me to give. But from now on I will smile more often. I'll do it for him.* "Thank you for telling me," she said aloud. "Your son must have been a good man in his heart. If there is anything I can do, please let me know." They both smiled at each other, for each knew that she had found a new friend.

The End"

"What a lovely story," Graham said. "Don't you think so, Telly?" he asked, turning to his friend. But Telly was crying like a baby. Tears were flowing in gushes down his screen and splashing off his metallic boots.

Doré produced a wad of tissues and dried his eyes. "You're likely to get a short circuit," she said. "By the way, I'd be delighted to have you join me for supper before you continue on your journey." With that, everyone went inside, with Telly asking question after question. After supper, everyone went out to the porch to talk. Graham sat on one of those swinging seats and became lost in thought as he swung gently back and forth. "Penny for your thoughts?" said Doré, sensing that the boy was a little sad.

"Oh, I was just wondering if I will ever find a way to get home. I think Oz is a very interesting place, with lots of incredibly wonderful people (except for that old Witch), but I am getting very homesick, and I miss my family terribly. Not only that, but they are probably worried sick and have probably called the police about their missing child."

"Well," replied Doré, "you just happen to be in the right place ... You see that old well where you quenched your thirst? Well, it's a wishing well. A real, true wishing well. And if you throw in a coin and make a sincere unselfish wish, your wish will come true instantly. Of course, you only get one guaranteed wish, but if you make a second wish, you have an eighty percent chance of that coming true, also."

Graham immediately perked up as Doré's words sank in. Then he became crestfallen as his eyes fell upon Telly's forlorn face, not to mention the disappointment reflected in the faces of the Cowardly Lion and the Hungry Tiger. He had made a wonderful new friend in Telly and was just getting to know the others, and now they were going to be separated—perhaps forever.

Doré, quickly realizing what the situation was, offered her condolences but assured Graham that if he were to make that second wish with great sincerity, there was a very good chance he could come back for a visit. With that, Graham shook hands with everyone and gave them each a big hug. He then threw a penny into the well as he made his two wishes. "I wish to go back home," and "I wish to come back to Oz someday for a visit." Then, as he waved goodbye to everyone, he slowly became invisible, only to reappear for a second, then slowly disappear again. This happened two or three times as Doré explained to Telly that the magic was working all right but that Graham's mixed feelings on the matter were delaying the final teleportation. Just then, there was a large black shadow overhead and a sudden WHOOSH! as a projectile whizzed past Graham's head. Back and forth it went, to reveal none other than the Wicked Witch on her broomstick, grabbing for Graham as she passed him.

"SO, LITTLE MAN. THOUGHT YOU'D ESCAPE FROM ME, EH? I DON'T THINK SO, MY FINE FEATHERED FRIEND!" She wailed like a banshee as she finally grabbed him by the shoulder and shook him as he desperately tried to escape. In the distance Graham fancied he could hear his mother's voice calling him.

"Graham! Graham!" His eyes—which had been shut tightly as the Witch shook him—opened to see with great surprise his mother's face as she also shook him. "Wake up! Wake up! Don't you know it's twelve midnight? And you haven't even done your homework! Your father will be having serious words with you in the morning, young man. Now, up to your room immediately!"

Graham had not been expecting to come home to such a tongue-lashing, but he was very happy to finally be back home after so many harrowing experiences. Ever since he had first been abducted to Oz, he had considered it his mission to get home again. The wishing well had made it possible.

But as Graham turned out the light beside his bed that night and laid his head against his pillow, he began to think over the events that he had experienced in Oz. Of course he had wanted to get home to his family. It only made sense that he would. He was only twelve and he needed them. Not only that, but they would be worried sick. He had made a sensible wish. Or had he? As he lay on his bed, it occurred to him that he might have used his penny to wish away the wicked witch and save Oz. A feeling of guilt began to gnaw at him. Had he actually used his penny to desert his friends when they needed him most? He realized then what a selfish act that had been. *Not entirely selfish,* he thought. *I was thinking of my family as much as myself.* But he knew that he was making excuses and that he should have wished more wisely. As he slowly drifted off into a troubled sleep, he saw images of the Cowardly Lion, the Hungry Tiger, Telly, Jeanne-Marie, MacDonald Lindsay, Doré, and many other Oz folk pass before his eyes.

The following day, Graham's mother was sorting the boy's dirty clothes for the wash when she noticed an ink stain on his shirt pocket. She checked the pocket and found a piece of paper with some kind of smudged drawing and words below the sketch that she could not make out without her reading glasses. It looked like, something … speare. Without a thought, she crumpled it up into a ball and threw it in the trash.